As a professional psychologist, I know well the value of therapeutic intervention and clinical care. These proven resources are space heaters compared to the furnace of human connection for melting the icy grip of isolation. In *I See You*, Julie Lee gives us a heartfelt invitation to peel back a few layers and truly connect with each other—lessons she learned at ground level. Her guidance here will heal hearts and open relationships in a way that is socially profound and psychologically sound.

—Paul H. Jenkins, PhD Psychologist, author of
Pathological Positivity, and host of *Live on Purpose TV*

In a world that moves too fast and argues too much, Julie Lee reminds us of the importance—and power—of human connection and compassion. In sharing her story with such authenticity, she empowers us to recognize the capacity for healing and the sense of purpose to be found in our own. *I See You* is a must-read for all who hope to see beyond the surface and into the heart of the human experience.

—Jennie Taylor, Civilian Aide to the Secretary of
the Army for the State of Utah, Gold Star Wife

The art of the human connection is alive! An impactful and invigorating look at why we need to not push away from each other, but instead encourage us to move in closer to each other and heal through compassion and connection. A message so badly needed with all the growing disconnect with others in politics, social media, and common issues we face everyday. Julie Lee captures beautifully how this significance can come in the simplest of moments of core human connection.

—Jon Petz, Business Leadership Keynote Speaker and
author of *Significance in Simple Moments*

Julie is one of the most relatable, empathetic people I have ever collaborated with. Julie shares her struggles with anxiety, depression, fear, and the unknown in such a raw, vulnerable way that those seeking motivation will feel seen and understood. She uses her gifts of energy, motivation, and compassion to show that healing and growth are possible despite the challenges that life throws our way.

—Tony Overbay, LMFT, host of *The Virtual Couch* Podcast

This is a true testament of the power of connection and compassion that is needed in all our lives. Julie Lee has beautifully outlined the miracles that can happen when we choose to see the potential and worth of every soul.

—Clint Pulver, Professional Drummer, Corporate Keynote Speaker, and author of *I Love It Here*

I have become a better person after reading *I See You* because it has changed the way that I think and act. As a business owner and leadership consultant I am aware of the complications, divisions, and isolations that exist in today's society. There has never been a more important time for individuals to "see" and connect with others. This timely and important book will teach you how to do that.

—Sydne Jacques, CEO of Jacques and Associates

In *I See You*, Julie Lee masterfully shows us how to engage emotionally to create happiness through connection. Introspection and self-growth are necessary to see others and truly appreciate them. Julie teaches us how to become our most authentic selves to be able to bring out the best in those around us.

—Ty Bennett, keynote speaker and author of *Partnership Is the New Leadership*

I SEE YOU

How compassion and connection save lives

JULIE LEE

PLAIN SIGHT PUBLISHING
An imprint of Cedar Fort, Inc.
Springville, Utah

© 2020 Julie Lee

ISBN 13: 978-1-4621-3808-1

Published by Plain Sight Publishing, an imprint of Cedar Fort, Inc.
2373 W. 700 S., Springville, UT 84663
Distributed by Cedar Fort, Inc., www.cedarfort.com

LIBRARY OF CONGRESS CONTROL NUMBER: 2020942182

Cover design by Wes Wheeler
Cover design © 2020 Cedar Fort, Inc.
Edited and typeset by Valene Wood

Printed in the United States of America

10 9 8 7 6 5 4 3 2 1

Printed on acid-free paper

Dedication

For Rob, who refused to let me sleep
on the bathroom floor alone. I have
never been loved so fiercely.

And for Amy, who taught me the
meaning of unconditional love by living
it. I will always be your story keeper.

Thank you for all
You do for Nebo. ♡
Much Love,
Julie Lee

Contents

CONTENTS

Foreword

Years ago, when I was first asked to join the child trafficking unit of Homeland Security, I had no idea what was involved. As I began investigating child trafficking, I was immersed in the underbelly of the beast, exposed to horrors that I never could have imagined and pray you never do.

I went home at night and held my children so tightly; I think they thought their dad was going crazy. I was completely overwhelmed. I was sure that I couldn't continue this line of work and my wife Katherine supported my decision to leave the department. After pondering for a few days and a lot of prayer, she convinced me that I needed to continue.

Realizing what a sheltered life I had lived, I began to develop real empathy for these little children who were being brutalized. I was devastated when I couldn't work certain cases because of our federal government jurisdictional restraints. Ultimately, that is the reason I left the government and started Operation Underground Railroad.

Because of the empathy I learned in my work at Homeland Security, I have dedicated my life to identify, find, and rescue trafficked children. Without empathy, I wouldn't have been able to find the motivation or desire to step into this world of darkness and evil.

It is far easier to close off our hearts, ears, and shut our eyes, all to protect ourselves from learning about the horrific realities experienced by many. We cannot do that to these children; we cannot shut them out. We must see those who are suffering in the darkness and bring them to the light.

Julie Lee embodies compassion and connection; she draws her conviction from personal life experiences with both darkness and light. She is a testament to the resilience of the individual. When Julie says "I See You" she is not just repeating a platitude; she really does *see* people in a way that many have forgotten. Not because people *can't* see, but mostly because people *don't want to.*

It can be terrifying to reach out from our own little worlds to help someone whose problems we don't understand and we can't fix. Why should we do it? Because our relationships are everything. The relationships we develop in our lifetime are the only things worth doing.

Our relationships last forever.

You can achieve success, riches, fame, and you will still feel unfulfilled if you are disconnected from the people around you.

Just decades ago, our world was very different. There were no skeletons in closets because the closets didn't have doors; everyone knew each other. People interacted on a community level.

In the complexities of today, you can live next to someone for ten years and know nothing about them if you choose. It shouldn't be that way.

As human beings, we are made to be social; without social interaction we get sick physically, mentally, and spiritually. The miracle is that compassion and connection have the ability to heal; I have witnessed it. At O.U.R., we rescue children from the worst kind of darkness; and they are *resilient.* When we place them in aftercare facilities, they begin to develop healthy meaningful relationships. They become new creatures—full of light that they then extend to others.

When we reach out and give, we find ourselves. Sometimes it is just sitting and listening to someone talk. We don't need to know the solution to their problems, we just need to listen.

Don't be afraid to care. Don't just read this book and forget the fire you felt. Accept it as a call to action and join the fight for good. Be a better member of your family, community, and society. Begin in your immediate family and start to heal the rifts that exist there.

I promise you that *seeing* others with compassion and connecting with them will be a transformative experience with rich rewards. You will start to see people in the same way Julie Lee strives to see people. Most important, the way God wants us to see each other.

—Tim Ballard

Introduction

Ialways saw myself writing a book, but not this one. When I was little, I used to say I wanted to be a children's book author. If someone had told me ten years ago that I would write a nonfiction book *period*, I would have turned around to see who they were talking to. And then the next decade happened and to quote my favorite actor, that was when *my life got flipped, turned upside down.* I'll leave the rapping to Will and get on with the writing.

If your first reaction to the title "I See You" was to think of a creepy stalker waving at you from the bushes, you're in good company. Rob felt the same way at first. When he wouldn't let me put an "I See You" sign on our wall because the idea of waking up to I SEE YOU every morning freaked him out, he really left me no choice but to randomly send him creepy screenshots throughout his workday. "I See You" written in blood on windshields, on barn doors—there were so many options. Google brings up all sorts of images with that phrase.

Rest assured this is not that kind of book. This is a book about the part you play in hope and healing.

I received an email from someone who compared the "I See You" message to an ICU, or intensive care unit, in a hospital. I like that. Healing happens in an ICU and my hope is that healing will occur in our lives as well as we learn to love better.

Everyone's life story has ups and downs and mine has been no different. I have known joy, peace, heartbreak, and suffering. What has made my life unique is not a shock-and-awe experience. No, what has made my life unique are the people who have willingly shown up in my best *and* worst moments. I have been impacted forever by individuals who chose to look at me with compassion and connect with me in pivotal moments. I cannot help myself; I have to tell the world why their examples matter.

My purpose in writing this book is to bring into stark clarity how badly we as a collective society need to engage with each other in a real, authentic way if we are to combat the onslaught of isolation, loneliness, and even suicide. We need to look each other in the eyes when we speak and touch each other on the shoulder when we greet. At worst, loneliness is a life or death situation, and at best, it creates an unsatisfactory life. I am confident that human compassion and connection is the antidote to our often disconnected culture.

The phrase "I See You" was first introduced to me by Brittney.

I was given Brittney's blog information by a mutual friend who thought the two of us could relate in our struggles with anxiety and depression. I binge-read Brittney's posts and sent her an email. After reassuring her that I wasn't trying to sell her an herbal supplement, she agreed to meet in person. Our friendship began as our kids fed ducks at the park. We talked about our worst moments, the mysteries of life, and hope for the future.

Ten months later, Brittney gave me a birthday present. It was a bracelet with the words "i see you" inscribed on it. Brittney wore a similar bracelet that she purchased months before at an Idina Menzel concert. She heard Idina's song *I See You* and knew I would appreciate the reminder it gives. These are some of the lyrics:

Here's to the lonely
To the broken-hearted
I want you to know I feel your pain
Here's to the hopeless
The almost forgotten

To those who got lost along the way
I see you, I see you, I see you
When you're alone
And you can't go back home
At the end of the day, I see you
I'll remember your face[1]

Brittney gave me the bracelet to remind me that I am always seen, that my life is never unnoticed. My life was witnessed by her, God, and so many others. It was one of the most meaningful gifts I have ever received.

I began noticing the phrase "I see you" in other places too.

For almost a decade, the film *Avatar (2009)* held the spot for highest grossing movie of all time. The film depicts a blue-skinned species named the Na'vi who populate a planet called Pandora. The Na'vi are fiercely loyal people who feel deeply. Throughout the film, the words "I see you" carry special significance. According to the director's Fandom site, "I see you" in the Na'vi language is regarded as a greeting "to express a positive feeling about meeting someone." It is more closely a synonym of "understand" or "comprehend." "To See" is a cornerstone of Na'vi philosophy. It is to open the mind and the heart to the present. Incidentally, the theme song of *Avatar* is entitled *I See You*, sung by Leona Lewis.

What does "I see you" mean to me? It means I am witnessing you and your life, right now, in real time. It means I look at you when we are talking, because you are worth my time and my focus. There is nothing you need to do, no requirements you need to meet to be deserving of my complete attention. Just simply breathe and you've done it.

Our society struggles to see each other. Not just teenagers addicted to social media, but grown adults—people who didn't have cell phones as kids. People like me and people like you.

I've noticed in the grocery store line that people often don't engage with me. They don't return my gaze or my smile. They don't look me in the eyes. Instead they look at their phones.

I had a therapist once ask me, "How did people do it in the olden days? How did they survive unspeakable grief, burying family members, enduring plagues and wars? How did they live with the heartache?"

She answered her own question; I'll never forget what she said.

"They did it *together*. They sent husbands and sons off to war *together*. They endured plagues *together*."

In contrast, the options to isolate and numb—all of which are within close reach—makes our era strikingly different. With countless distractions available to us (shows to watch, articles to read, posts to comment on, pornography to view, and food to eat), the juxtaposition of real and cyber is messing with our heads. Many people don't know how to communicate in person anymore because they are accustomed to a virtual reality where communication skills are rarely necessary.

Why does isolation work so well? Feeling alone often leads to a lack of motivation and even depression. I can tell you from my first-hand experience that depression is a demanding mistress. Depression wants us alone, in the dark, where it's cold. Most important, depression wants us in a place where no one else can talk to us and remind us what's real. In a *hole* with no way out.

How do we save people from *the hole*? We see each other with compassion and form authentic, human connections in the present.

It is inspiring when someone stands in front of us and says, "I went through something hard and now I am better off for it."

But what about the person listening who is in the middle of a crisis and doesn't see a way?

We need to do more than *inspire* each other; we need to *relate* to each other.

While I will share personal experiences to help illustrate important principles, this book is not *my* story. It is ours. This is our story, the complex, beautiful human race. I have met people who come from a variety of life circumstances, and they each have their own powerful narrative. A man who escaped a scientology cult. A professional drummer who was bullied because he couldn't keep his hands still. A White House Secret Service Officer with a stutter. Each has told me the same thing that I am about to tell you.

We need each other, you and I. We thrive at home, at work, and at play when we strive for compassion and connection in our relationships.

If we can recognize the fog that keeps us from seeing others, we can discover the light that illuminates the people around us. We each have gifts that are innately ours. We have those gifts to help us truly see each other, to save each other from isolated lives.

Compassion and connection save lives. I watched it happen. Not from far away, but up close and personal. It happened to me. My life was saved again and again by ordinary people *seeing* me. They were there on my very worst days, cradling me in my suffering; they were there again on my best days, celebrating my victories. We need each other. We can do this life. But we have to do it together.

I see you. I witness your life. It's an honor to have you here, in these pages, with me. I love you already.

Thank you for reading this book.

Julie Lee

Part One

The Rallying Cry

Chapter 1

Do You See Me?

Your life will not go unnoticed because I will notice it. Your life will not go unwitnessed because I will be your witness.[2]

—*Shall We Dance?*

When you are too panicked and depressed to eat or sleep, cleaning the bathrooms is the first thing to go.

Lying face down on the filthy tile floor of my bathroom, I willed my mouth to say the same prayer I had been praying for months. "Please God, please. Come and heal me. I'll do anything. Save me, God. Please. I've done everything I can. Please."

The anxiety and depression I experienced was crippling; I needed relief.

I wanted to die. Not because I didn't want to live. My three people, my little family, they were the only reason I needed to stay alive. Yet, I didn't see how I could survive another day of this hell, before some animal instinct within me would take over and end the suffering. The thought terrified me.

I heard stories of people who were institutionalized for poor mental health; my greatest relief came from imagining that I could be one of them. I had begged Rob to take me somewhere, somewhere where they would lock me in a room and give me the official PTSD diagnosis that my therapist suspected. A place where I would paint watercolor flowers and meet in support groups with strangers like me. A place that would fix me. I dreamt of coming home a new woman, who was invincible against the mental ailment I had become so familiar with.

Just down the hall from the bathroom, my little boy and even littler girl, only eighteen months apart, sat playing in our living room. Lydia was squished in the Bumbo; her delicious thighs were getting too fat to fit in the seat. Sam loved making her laugh. He imitated my husband and I, making silly two-year-old faces and shaking toys in front of her face.

Those kids, *my babies*, were everything to us. It had taken Rob and me years to have children. When they went to bed at night, we often sat and looked at the pictures we had taken of them on our phones that day. Our kids were our obsession.

As a child, I watched my parents battle my father's mental illness. The thought of affecting my kids, the way I was affected as a child, was more than my heart could take. What about Rob? I was so different from the spunky college girl he had married. I saw myself becoming the mentally unstable spouse that I swore I'd never marry.

A hard worker and optimist at heart, I had always known I would have a happy life. While I had watched my own father suffer from years of clinical depression, I had never seen that darkness in myself. I was bubbly, ultra-motivated, and an expert avoider of all things depression. As a teenager, I had promised myself that no matter what happened in life, I would *force myself not to be depressed.*

Well here I was, age twenty-seven, on the bathroom floor again, having done everything I could think of to heal myself. I'd been fighting anxiety and depression on and off for the past six years, and I refused to believe it was tougher than me. Countless times, I had googled "how to heal from depression" and scavenged the lists, checking off each task one by one. I ate healthy, exercised, served, meditated, worshiped, read all the books, smelled all the oils—heck, I'd even learned a new instrument to try to cure me.

But like so many afternoons before, I collapsed in front of the toilet, with the fan blowing so my kids wouldn't hear my sobs. It was important to me that they remain completely oblivious to their mother, enduring yet another day in her isolated, psychological hell.

In the Bible, there are multiple accounts of a story about a woman who has a physical illness involving blood. She tries all sorts of things to find healing, but nothing works. For twelve years she suffers, until she sees Jesus walking down the road. Pushing through the crowd, she reaches out her hand and touches the corner of His robe. In that moment, she is healed; her faith in Jesus is enough to make her whole again.

I knew the Bible. I believed in Jesus.

I stretched out my arms across the ground as far as I could, almost touching the tub, and I begged Jesus Himself to appear before me so that I could touch His robe. I told God that I had the faith to be healed, and I think I did. But He didn't come.

And I wasn't healed.

No person, no burst of lightning, and no Higher Power came to release me from my nightmare of a reality. Not yet.

***

I have questions for you, reader.

Do you see me?

A fellow human being, collapsed on the floor; do you connect with my cry for relief?

Can you picture me in your mind?

Have you ever felt that desperate?

Is there *anything* that would hold you back from getting down on that floor with me?

Would you feel too embarrassed to get close to me, where I can see your face?

Would you back away slowly out of insecurity?

Would you care what my political views were, my sexual orientation, or my religion?

Most of us want to help, but often don't. We back away, telling ourselves someone else will help, someone who is more equal to the task. We have good intentions, but unfortunately our good intentions don't help the person on the floor.

Our own insecurities and differences can hold us back from seeing each other. If we don't understand these obstacles that get in the way, we will never change. I know this because I used to feel the same helplessness.

I once saw someone crying in a public hallway, someone who was clearly in emotional turmoil. What did I do? I found a different route to my destination, far away from the crying that was making me feel uncomfortable.

I did nothing.

It wasn't until *I* was the one sobbing in public that I realized how wrong I had been. I realized how stupid and irrelevant my need to be comfortable really was.

Visiting *the hole* will teach you that.

I have been interviewed many times about my experiences with anxiety and depression. I remember a specific interview. Tony Overbay, a licensed marriage and family therapist was interviewing me for his podcast, *The Virtual Couch*. There was a moment in our interview when I became emotional as he expressed empathy for his clients. Tony described what it's like to sit across from someone who is suicidal. "We want you to live. That is our ultimate goal," he said. "It just breaks my heart that sometimes people have to get to that point before they feel like they are enough." I was reminded why I care so much about this mission of *I See You*. When people need us, it should be all hands on deck. At the end of the day, nothing else matters more than keeping people here.

An article was published this year in the *Harvard Business Review* stating, "Depression is the leading cause of disability worldwide. One in five Americans is affected by mental health issues, with depression being the most common problem. A recent report by Blue Cross Blue Shield found that depression diagnoses are rising at a faster rate for millennials and teens than for any other generation."

Unique to this period of history, are the severe epidemics no one can see. The stakes are high, and the results are frightening. Anxiety, depression, and suicide are among them. Isolation is permeating every family, company, school, and religion. It is everyone's problem.

I know what it feels like to not want to be here. Those feelings are real. I can say with certainty that the solution to isolation is human compassion and connection.

There are a lot of people who experience loneliness and isolation without ever becoming clinically depressed or anxious. Instead, they feel upset, dissatisfied, and unmotivated. When we stop connecting, for whatever reason, we see painful consequences.

There are countless distractions keeping us from engaging with each other. Connecting with people in today's climate has to be an intentional choice.

Many of us are a little lost right now. We are somewhat disconnected from reality. We are not quite sure what's real and what to believe. These are some of the natural consequences of having access to an abundance of information and virtual options. At night, I find myself wanting to scroll through Facebook rather than have a conversation with my husband; exhaustion is an enemy to effort. Sometimes we want to be numb to "unfeel" the sensitivity of life. It's easy to choose a virtual reality over a regular one, and we are suffering because of those choices.

To lead meaningful, rich lives, you and I need to connect and see each other with compassion. It is our duty as human beings to take care of each other. In one of my favorite books, *Daring Greatly*, shame researcher Brené Brown says, "Connection is why we're here; it is what gives purpose and meaning to our lives!"[3]

Choosing connection over isolation means our quality of life is about to get a whole lot better. My life dramatically shifted when I started choosing connection over isolation. I began to recognize that I had an irreplaceable part to play in the human family at large. I started celebrating my differences instead of hating them. Most important, I was able to see that I was not alone.

There are a lot of things that can get in the way of connecting with other people, especially people who are different from us. Snap judgements, belief systems, and economic status just to name a few. But when we think about that mother on the bathroom floor, begging God to take away the pain, all the differences we have become one hundred percent obsolete.

I love the pairing of compassion and connection. They complement each other and work hand in hand. When we form a connection with another human being, the byproduct is usually feeling a greater amount of compassion for them. We judge them less harshly because we see them as complex human beings, rather than problems. It's easy to dislike someone from far away where we can't see the circumstances they are coming from. It's a whole lot harder when we are close up and see what's really going on with them. So my challenge for us is this:

Let's not look away. Let's not close our eyes. If we look, we will find what needs to be done. I wrote this book to help us find ways to do just that. But no book, podcast, or article can tell us exactly what to do. Not the way our own soul and conscience can. We all have to find moments to be still and to ponder what it is *we* are meant to be and who *we* are meant to save. For me, I felt like I should write this book, so I'm doing it.

It's important that we are patient with ourselves throughout this process of seeing. Agonizing over the past and worrying about the future will suck away time we could spend *living* today. We have to clear out distraction. Then, let our heart and soul lead our life with intention. If we listen and look for ways we can live with stronger connections and greater compassion for others, we will become a kinder, happier people. Our life is going to change and we will never regret shifting our gaze to who is right in front of us. I have seen this compassion work in my own life and in the lives of the angels surrounding me.

The Bottom Line

Isolation is permeating our world, but we can make intentional changes to "see" each other with compassion and connection. Our ability to thrive is dependent on our ability to connect with others, which will undoubtedly lead to a greater amount of compassion for them.

Do you remember that young mother on the dirty, bathroom floor? Don't forget about her.

Chapter 2

Whoville Needs Us

Every Who down in Who-ville liked Christmas a lot, But the Grinch, who lived just north of Who-ville, Did NOT![4]

—*How the Grinch Stole Christmas*

At the Lee house, *How the Grinch Stole Christmas* is big news. I was excited to share the story with my kids, but I made the mistake of exposing them too early. In my excitement, I showed Sam a clip of the Jim Carrey version when he was only two years old. He cried and has refused the movie ever since.

I eventually talked Sam into watching the original 1966 version with me, which he tolerated. I probably should have started with that one. In 2018, another version came out in theatres. Sam refused. But as fate would have it, he saw the film at my sister's house with the rest of his cousins while the adults were playing games. Good old peer pressure; gotta love it. Afterward he told me with a grin, "Mom it was SOOO silly!" I caught myself and didn't say *I told you so* like a six-year-old. I was happy that someone got him to watch the dang movie, even if it wasn't me. And that's how my kids' obsession with the movie began.

They told everyone about it, as if it had just come out in theatres, instead of two years ago. Rob and I appreciated the hip hop music and witty humor. It could have been worse. It could have been a *My Little Pony* obsession. Thank heavens; I was spared.

For Halloween, we used a lot of green and brown face paint to make Sam a convincing Grinch, and Lydia, his sidekick, Max the dog. Rob and I were happy for an excuse to wear pajamas, as Cindy-Lou Who and Who Boy #1.

During the months of *The Grinch* craze, mornings consisted of my kids dumping out their Duplos and reinventing the scenes from the movie. One side of the living room became the Grinch's cave (Sam called it his "cage," which has interesting implications), and the other side became Whoville. Next, The Grinch (a designated duplo man with black hair and glasses), flew on his rocket ship/sleigh/racecar to steal Christmas from the Whos. He loaded up his vehicle with all things Christmas and took it back to the cave. The storyline was flexible at this point, and it changed as time went on. Sometimes the Grinch had a change of heart and returned Christmas, and other times a monster showed up to eat all of the characters.

The *real* plotline of *How the Grinch Stole Christmas* is slightly different. The Grinch is a green, hairy misfit who lives in a cave above Whoville—a community that is fanatical about Christmas. The Grinch hates Christmas culture. In a rage, he decides to steal Christmas, disguised as Santa Claus. During the heist, he meets a kind, small Who child, Cindy Lou Who. He is undeterred. The next morning, having arrived home with his sleigh full of the stolen Christmas goodies, he hears something unexpected. Despite their stolen possessions, the Whos are *singing* together. The Grinch is baffled, then touched, and his heart is changed. He returns everything he stole, and even joins the Whos for their Christmas feast.

The Grinch didn't belong up on the mountain; and neither do we. We are sorely needed in Whoville.

REASONS FOR THE CAVE

> Staring down from his cave with a sour, Grinchy frown
> At the warm lighted windows below in their town.[5]

One reason I like the Grinch's character so much is because I can relate to him. Like the Grinch, sometimes I want to stay up on my mountain. I'm not mad at anybody; I just want to do my own thing. I want my lavender mist and my meditation space, all in a place that I can control. In a lot of ways, the seclusion of a cave makes sense.

But why did the Grinch move up to the cave in the first place? The original book doesn't give us much backstory of the Grinch's life, but one movie version does.

In the Jim Carrey adaptation, the Grinch experiences flashbacks from his troubled past. In his memories, he is mocked and humiliated, making him self-conscious about his appearance.

One reason people isolate themselves from a group, community, or even family, is because of negative experiences they have had in the past. They may feel hurt by something that happened, or make assumptions about the way people feel about them. Whether their interpretations are accurate or false doesn't matter. Our mind is our reality. Like the Grinch, I have gotten burned before; I've had my heart broken by someone I should have been able to trust. I understand the pull of the cave, where no one can hurt you again.

In high school, I was an outgoing girl; I did the student council thing and I had friends in all sorts of different groups. But still, there were groups I didn't try to breach because I thought I wouldn't be liked and was afraid of humiliating myself. Some of that might have been true. There *are* mean people out there; they exist.

In Jim Carrey's *How the Grinch Stole Christmas*, there are Who children who are legitimately mean to the young Grinch. In my mind, he partly leaves Whoville to avoid being hurt again; by self-protecting, he disconnects. But the problem is, he never comes back down. His feelings fester over time.

Sometimes we isolate when we have been mistreated or we feel self-conscious. We hole up in a proverbial cave. We might check social media and think we know what's going on in Whoville, just like the

Grinch could hear the Christmas music. But that's not real connection. It is possible to be in a room full of people and feel completely alone. There is a way to be in a cave mentally and emotionally, and physically reside in Whoville. Remember, Hell is not a place; it's a state of mind.

FINDING QUIET

Oh, the noise! Oh, the noise! Noise! Noise! Noise! NOISE!
That's one thing he hated! The NOISE! NOISE! NOISE! NOISE![6]

I feel you, Grinch.

As we try to see others, something we all need is quiet time for ourselves. As our environment gets louder, our minds can become overactive. It's difficult to calm my mind down unless my surroundings are quiet too. But even though it's loud sometimes, I don't want to abandon Whoville.

I'm not living in my Who-house alone. One of the hardest things for me about getting married and becoming a parent was not being able to control my space. Having scattered toys and an unmade bed drives me up the wall. I have an outward-processor for a husband and two very loud children; lots of noise happens in this corner of Whoville.

When everything feels too loud, a cave all by myself where I can control everything sounds pretty nice. But I have learned that I don't thrive in caves, or *holes* for that matter. I would rather have noise to handle, than the cold silence of depression. Depression follows isolation like a cat you made the mistake of feeding. No, I will never move up to a cave to escape the noise. I will take a break instead.

People ask me, how do you keep your house so tidy? I find a way because it's a survival tactic. When my physical environment is chaotic, my mind is chaotic. It's a bad combination. In my corner of Whoville, I get a say. I keep an orderly house because it increases my quality of life, my ability to thrive, and my capacity to help others. In my house, I have a tub to soak in, peppermint oil to rub on my temples, and countless books I want to read. I have fuzzy blankets and good food to eat.

I love my set up in Whoville because I have made it a place where I can find quiet. I have learned to take intentional breaks every day; I have learned to find stillness. Finding quiet is essential if we want to invite others into our lives.

I love inviting my fellow Whos into my house; I love singing songs with them and celebrating our lives together. I don't invite everybody into my home, but most people I do.

We need never feel alone in Whoville.

HOW HEARTS GROW

Well . . . in Who-ville they say
That the Grinch's small heart
Grew three sizes that day![7]

What made our green friend change?

First, Cindy Lou Who made an impression on him. He created a *connection* with another human being. Not by looking at Cindy Lou Who via her Instagram account @christmasorbust; he met her face-to-face. It's hard to hate someone close up. When we don't like someone, if we move in closer we usually find that our compassion increases. Compassion inspires change.

Second, the Grinch realizes that the Whos were not who he thought they were. His negative experience as a kid had been simmering for a long time, which only exaggerated his hatred towards the Whos. In his mind, they were shallow and cared only about *things*. When the Grinch heard the Whos singing Christmas morning, he realized that he had underestimated them.

Sometimes we are wrong about people. Sometimes people change. Whos who were previously mean to the Grinch, changed. Their examples inspired the Grinch to change as well.

Our Whoville is made up of all sorts of crazy people, including you and me. We all have baggage, we all have quirks, and we are all *needed* in Whoville. We can't engage with other people if we are holed up in a cave on the mountain, looking at everyone else's life through a screen of never-ending social media posts. We are no help to anyone from way up there.

If you're camped up on the mountain, it's time to come down. Build a fence. Build sound-proof walls, that's all fine. We need you down in Whoville, where no one ever needs to feel alone.

The Bottom Line

Seeing people means engaging with them in close emotional proximity. While distancing ourselves may feel safe, our happiness grows when we intentionally connect with others.

Chapter 3

We're Not Alone

There's a place where we don't have to feel unknown.[8]

—*Dear Evan Hansen*

One of my gifts is that I can't keep my mouth shut.

If I'm having a bad day, my sisters usually know about it because I'm on the phone with one of them, crying it out one dramatic detail at a time. Sometimes you need to just kick that horse over and over again to make sure it's really dead. I'm good at calling out when I'm distressed.

A few years ago, I was in the middle of a particularly awful morning. I was stuck alone with my anxious thoughts and two screaming kids. I reached out to a new friend of mine, who offered to help me clean my house. She swept my floors and scrubbed my countertops, as I cried doing the dishes.

Before she left, we sat on my living room couch and I told her what was going on with me. She didn't try to talk over me or explain away my pain. She looked me in the eyes and simply listened. Then she asked if she could show me something; it was a picture of her beautiful stillborn son who was delivered a few years prior. I cried when I saw the photo. I wasn't the only one who knew about suffering. My friend and I related to each other because we both knew

21

something about pain. Our goodbye hug felt a little more real when she left my house that morning.

My friend didn't show me the picture of her baby to compare hardships. She showed it to me to say, "I see you." I was vulnerable with her by inviting her into my home on a day when I was far from my best. My willingness to be seen gave her silent permission to be vulnerable and share her heart with me in return.

My friend taught me something valuable that day.

I had been feeling alone, I had been feeling like no one could understand. I was wrong. I wasn't unique in feeling pain; other people could relate to my pain because of their own, distinct experiences. I was beginning to identify one of the ugliest lies ever told:

I AM ALONE.

That's a lie. None of us are alone.

We're not alone if we're divorced. We're not alone if we're addicted to prescription drugs and haven't found a way to stop. We aren't alone if we have infertility problems or if we've been bullied. We aren't alone if we're gay, if we've lost a child, or if we have made mistakes—big mistakes.

We might believe we are the only one who has had the challenges we've had. *No one understands. No one gets it. No one will love us if they see our weaknesses.*

We're not alone; everyone has both challenges and weaknesses. When we think we are alone, we tend to close up and isolate ourselves from people.

THE LONELINESS OF HARD

Hard is hard. The challenges we experience are sacred and ours alone. Certainly, there will be times when our road will feel lonely, even when others are willing to help.

My brother, Eric, found out his two-year-old daughter had Leukemia in the middle of his college semester. Shortly after she was diagnosed, he was forced to return to campus to get something. He walked into the engineering building where his classmates were studying for upcoming exams. He had spent countless hours collaborating, laughing, and bonding with these people. Yet, he felt a wave of shock as he watched them go about life as if nothing had happened. His impulse was to scream, "How can you think studying is important when my baby girl could be dying?!" Eric felt distant from his classmates as he realized their lives were moving forward.

There is nothing wrong with mourning the life we thought we'd have; mourning is healthy. However, if we compare our challenges with others, resentment and isolation can increase.

COMPARING CHALLENGES

As Eric's family continued to grow, each child brought a new health crisis. His routine became sleeping on hospital couches, starting IVs at home, and watching oxygen monitors. He struggled to connect with people who seemed to have a "normal" life. He couldn't relate to buying a house, going on vacations, and other typical life events that for him, were now on pause. As he listened to someone else's experiences, he couldn't help but compare them to his; he was perceiving their struggles through the lens of his own. In his mind, everyone else's challenges were about him.

As we've talked, Eric has realized that comparing challenges makes him feel alone. As he seeks to understand and listen—without interjecting his own experiences—he feels connected to the people around him.

If we assume that we are alone, then how can we ever have the kind of empathy for others that we want to have? We might not be able to *see* people for who they really are.

If I assume I'm alone because I have experienced infertility, how can I have empathy when my friend confides in me about her fear of an unexpected pregnancy? I could justify the thought, *you wouldn't complain as much if you were me.*

And . . . BAM. I am refusing both compassion and connection.

My tunnel vision takes over and I isolate instead of nurturing a relationship. I could have *seen* someone; instead, I pulled back, hurting both of us.

Believing we are alone can keep us from connecting to others, but realizing that we are *together* can unify us all.

WE'RE TOGETHER

It's exciting to find out we aren't alone because of the challenges we've endured. We can find friends everywhere. People with different backgrounds can become welcome guests in our circle of confidants.

If we assume our neighbor has a life of ease, we're probably wrong. We usually can relate to them easier than we think. People all around us want connection and compassion. We are in this life together and as humans, we want to be seen.

We can make all sorts of friends.

We will know how to treat people by learning how to treat ourselves first. When we learn to see ourselves with compassion, we come to the table equipped with skills that help us see others.

The Bottom Line

"I am alone" is a lie. Believing that lie keeps us from seeing others and ourselves accurately. The antidote to this lie is connection with others and the compassion that comes from seeing them up close and personal.

Part Two

Saving Ourselves First

Chapter 4

Self-Compassion

Failure is the opportunity to begin again more intelligently.[9]

—Henry Ford, founder, Ford Motor Company

I failed a test once. Well, more than once actually, but today I'm writing about the most important one I failed. It was an online quiz that tested my self-compassion. "This is the lowest score I've ever seen," the therapist (who made me take it) said. The self-hate talk had been in my head for so long, I didn't even know it was there.

I was about to embark on a journey to explore the unfamiliar and life-changing tool of being kind to myself, which would change the way I see people forever.

WHAT IS SELF-COMPASSION?

Self-compassion is extending compassion to ourselves in moments of pain or failure.

In her TED Talk *The Space Between Self-Esteem and Self-Compassion*, Dr. Kristin Neff explains, "Self-compassion is not a way of judging ourselves positively, self-compassion is a way of relating to ourselves kindly, embracing ourselves as we are, flaws and all."[10]

As someone who thrives on getting things done, I used to think being kind to myself would make me underperform. Until I tried it myself, I had no idea that being kind to ourselves makes us *more* motivated, not less.

TOOLS

There are many well-researched tools we can use to invoke more self-compassion in our lives. One tool is writing a letter to ourselves for times when we are struggling to treat ourselves kindly. It is powerful to read in our own handwriting, words of self-love and understanding when we don't want to give ourselves either.

Another tool for developing self-compassion is keeping a positive mantra close to our hearts. A mantra is a phrase we can repeat to ourselves frequently to help us stay focused on what we want; we can repeat the phrase to ourselves anytime self-hate rears its head. When I first began struggling with my mental health, I tried to picture the version of me that was years down the road, who had already overcome the challenges I was facing. I liked to think that my future self could see me and believed in me. My mantra became, "She's rooting for you." In moments when we lacked self-compassion, mantras can comfort us.

Developing self-compassion will enable us to extend that same compassion to others. In my experience, the most critical tool to master is talking to ourselves the way we talk to a good friend.

HOW WE TALK TO A FRIEND

Talking to ourselves how we talk to a friend takes intention. When self-defeating thoughts invade our mind, we can choose to respond the way we would to a buddy. For example, if we have the thought, "I'm a bad person," we can change it to "I made a mistake and that's okay." Talking back to our negative thoughts becomes natural with consistent practice. Compassion, not shaming, inspires change.

A few days ago, I left the stovetop on. My husband walked down the stairs and asked if something was burning; I realized my mistake and turned off the burner. Instead of telling myself I was stupid, I told myself the same truth I would tell a friend: "Everyone makes mistakes and it's okay. I'll be more careful next time." Instead of beating myself up, I resolved to pay closer attention while cooking.

THE MESSY HOUSE PRINCIPLE

One day, my friend brought her kids over for a playdate and my house was messy. As we chatted in my cluttered living room, I apologized for the mess. She waved away my apology and said, "No problem."

A few days later, I showed up at her house with my kids for yet another playdate. Her living room was littered with toys and books. She followed the unspoken standard of hosts and said, "Sorry about the mess."

I said, "Don't worry about it!"

This is the moment where I tell you the truth about me. I am a hypocrite. And so is my friend.

If it's *really* no big deal that my friend's house is dirty, then why do I apologize for mine? If she doesn't mind my house being cluttered, then why is she apologizing for hers?

When we apologize for a messy house, we are insinuating that a messy house is a sign of weakness. That it deserves an apology. We can't have the apology without the verdict.

When we go easy on ourselves for a messy house, we're more likely to extend that same compassion to other people in their messy houses.

SELF-COMPASSION CREATES HEALING

Hating our bodies is a universal issue. Dieting is a huge industry; there are a lot of men and women who hate themselves for how they look.

When I'm in a group setting and I call myself "fat," what am I communicating to the other people in that group? The girlfriend next to me, (who is bigger than me) says she *should lose a few pounds too*. I respond, *No way! You look great.*

We can guess how that friend might be feeling. If I'm speaking negatively about my body size, what does that say about her bigger body? My lack of self-compassion can leave her feeling insecure.

When we speak negatively about ourselves, we invite everyone else in the room to do the same.

On the flip side, when we are positive and accepting of ourselves, we are giving others permission to live with self-love too. Our self-compassion creates a safe space where others are comfortable in their own skin. Within that safe space, people can open up and be vulnerable with us, knowing that compassion is waiting. Practicing self-compassion does wonders to create trusting connections with others.

Exercise is an area that many struggle to practice self-compassion. My workout buddy works hard at it. She's learned how far to push her body without overexerting it. She knows it's okay to take a day off when her body is tired. When I told her that I left the gym after five minutes because my muscles were too sore, she congratulated me on listening to my body and giving it the break it needed. She has taught me that exercising with self-compassion does not mean making excuses; it means living with integrity about what your body needs that day. She has inspired me to exercise out of gratitude for my body.

It is with this same self-compassion that we can listen to ourselves and fulfill our own needs.

TAKING CARE OF OUR NEEDS

Seeing ourselves—accepting, forgiving, and loving ourselves, with all our human weaknesses—makes it easier to see others.

Sometimes we put our own needs on the bottom of our to-do list. We want to help others and may even think it is noble to neglect our own needs. While serving others is important, if we consistently place our needs last, we can feel burned out and angry—and that isn't helpful to anyone.

Taking care of our own needs is one of the best things we can do for the people we love. I try to exercise and read every single morning before my family wakes up. When I do, I have more to give and I tackle my day with confidence and joy.

Will there be times when we need to put someone else's needs above our own? Yes. Babies need to be fed and work deadlines need to be met. Taking care of our needs doesn't mean we sluff off responsibility—it means we fill our own cup so we have plenty to extend to others.

As Tara Brach wrote, "Feeling compassion for ourselves in no way releases us from the responsibility for our actions. Rather it releases us from the self-hatred that prevents us from responding to our life with clarity and balance."[11]

SELF-COMPASSION HELPS US *SEE*

I found Dr. Neff's research on motivation and happiness astounding. I love the connection she made between self-compassion and being able to see others. She says, "Where self-esteem asks how am I *different* than others, self-compassion asks how am I the *same* as others? To be human means to be imperfect. We make it so much worse by feeling we're isolated in our suffering and our imperfection, when in fact that's precisely what connects us to other people. The more we are able to keep our hearts open to ourselves, the more we have available to give to others."[12]

I have seen how the self-hate talk in my head can make me crankier towards my spouse. When I am disappointed in myself that I didn't get the dishes done, I'm more likely to get mad at Rob for not doing the dishes. When I tell myself it's okay to take a break from the dishes and relax, I don't feel angry if Rob's doing the same. Rob likes it when I'm nice to myself, because that means I'm nicer to him too.

When we stop equating success with how hard we work, we're more able to take care of both ourselves and others. One of my favorite poems illustrates self-compassion. I first heard it while meditating in a yoga class. The tears fell. Now it has a home in my office.

It is called "She Let Go," by Safire Rose. Some of my favorite lines read,

> She let go.
> No one was around when it happened.
> There was no applause or congratulations.

No one thanked her or praised her.
No one noticed a thing.
Like a leaf falling from a tree, she just let go.
There was no effort.
There was no struggle . . .
In the space of letting go, she let it all be.[13]

Developing self-compassion prepares us to give to others and to receive the love they have to offer in return.

The Bottom Line

Practicing self-compassion leads to inner-peace and *seeing* others better. When we talk to ourselves like we would a friend and take care of our own needs, it is easier to extend the same compassion to others.

Chapter 5

Giving and Receiving

There is generosity in giving, but gentleness in receiving.[14]

—Freya Stark

Four years ago, my sister, Amy, was diagnosed with breast cancer. She also found out she was pregnant with her sixth child; that was a lot of news at once. Everyone was shocked and the situation seemed impossible. How would she have surgery and endure chemotherapy, all while having an infant in-utero? How would she care for her other five children? How would she get through radiation treatments with a newborn? Her family needed help. In baptism-by-fire fashion, she and her husband Ryan, became well-acquainted with receiving.

Ryan was overwhelmed with gratitude. He made sincere efforts to thank those who helped his family. After their son was safely born and Amy finished her cancer treatments, Ryan looked for ways to help others. It brought him joy to serve, especially after receiving so much service himself. However, his help was often refused by the same people who had helped his family. It was painful when they refused his help. "When they turn me away, what are they saying about the help *I've* accepted? About all the times I have accepted *their* help?" Ryan asked me.

When those who supported Ryan refused his help, he felt like he'd been *taking* from them, instead of gracefully *receiving*. On the flip side, when he was able to serve someone who served his family, the experience filled him with increased gratitude and love. Gratitude for his ability to help, and love for the person he was helping.

In her lecture "The Anatomy of Trust," Brené Brown says this about trusting relationships, "I can fall apart, ask for help, and be in struggle, without being judged by you, and you can do the same with me. If you cannot ask for help, and they cannot reciprocate, that is not a trusting relationship. Real trust doesn't exist unless help is reciprocal in non-judgement."[15]

When someone serves me but won't let me serve them, I feel uncomfortable asking them for help in the future. Consciously or not, it appears they see my vulnerability as a drawback.

When someone offers us help and we *consistently* refuse their help—because *we can do it on our own* or *we don't want to bother them*—we are inherently communicating that it's a sign of weakness to accept help.

A RECEIVING RELATIONSHIP

There is nothing like receiving someone else's sacrifice in real time. Not long ago, Rob and I received difficult news in the form of a phone call. Word spread. A friend in my neighborhood showed up on my doorstep with a twelve-pack of Diet Dr. Pepper. Talk about seeing me, she could have easily left it on the doorstep with or without a note; I would have appreciated it. But instead, she rang the doorbell and told me, "I'm sorry you are sad. I brought you a treat." She gave me the opportunity to look at her and say "Thank you. Thank you for seeing me today." We were friends before this, but we were even better friends after.

I don't feel indebted to her. I don't feel that I *owe* her something. I feel gratitude that she saw me when I was hurting. Period. The love I felt from her encourages me to follow her example to *see* others, including her. If I take her cookies out of gratitude, so be it. It's not about paying back; it's about getting in each other's lives and saying *I*

SEE YOU. I see you over there, hurting alone in your house. I see you. You are not alone.

If we want to help others, we need to let others help us. Relationships where both parties give *and* receive provide opportunities for connection.

ANONYMOUS GIVING

There are many good reasons to give anonymously. In the Bible, Jesus taught, "But when you give to someone in need, don't let your left hand know what your right hand is doing." If it feels most appropriate to give anonymously, we might be right! However, we might consider that the person receiving our gift could benefit from knowing *who* saw them that day. *We* care about them and *we* are someone they can trust.

Ryan explained to me, "As much as I appreciated the anonymous gifts left on our porch, it meant so much to me when someone would look me in the eyes, shake my hand, and give to me openly. I was able to *receive* instead of just *take* by saying 'thank you' to the giver. It created a connection that strengthened our relationship. I know that *they* love my family and they know that *I* love them for it."

Giving isn't about *us*; giving is about making sure people know their lives are witnessed *by us*. Giving is about seeing each other.

Having said all that, I still think we get points in heaven for all good-intentioned giving.

GIVING AT A HEALTHY DISTANCE

When we don't know what someone needs because we don't know them well, it's a good idea to ask someone who does.

A former classmate of mine was killed, leaving his wife with one small child and another on the way. My heart ached for this new widow. She had also been a classmate, and although we didn't have a close relationship, I wanted to do something for her. I put together a package and then wondered how I should give it to her. Would she want a visitor? I reached out to her best friend, who expressed gratitude for my sensitivity and suggested I leave it on the doorstep. While this young widow was grateful for the outpouring of love from her community, she was emotionally exhausted from all the visits, sometimes from complete strangers, who came to weep with her.

I attached a card with my phone number to the package and then dropped it off on her doorstep. The gift had no strings attached. She had many close family and friends to lean on, but I wanted her to know I was available if she needed me.

It wasn't about *me*; it was about making sure *she* felt seen.

While we strive to be sensitive in these situations, in my experience, most people forgive us when we get it wrong. When someone is hurting, we just need to show up *somehow*—even if we do it badly. We can't let the wounded wonder if they are alone.

The Bottom Line

To build a trustworthy connection with someone, we need to be willing to receive help. By giving *and* receiving, we illustrate that receiving is strength, not weakness. We help others feel seen by thoughtfully giving.

Chapter 6

Replacing Comparison

*We won't be distracted by comparison
if we are captivated with purpose.*[16]

—Bob Goff

STAYING IN OUR LANE

When I first learned to drive, I had a bad habit of driving whatever direction my eyes were looking. When I looked to the left, my hands on the steering wheel automatically shifted to the left too, causing me to drift into the lane next to me. My driver's ed teacher swore at me a lot.

I realized quickly that if I wanted to get a driver's license, I was going to have to observe the traffic around me without driving into it. I had to focus on *staying in my own lane* to arrive at my destination safely.

We each are driving in our own lane, on our own life's path, and we need to stay in our own lane to avoid accidents. What does it look like to stay in our own lane? I was inspired by an experience my friend had last year.

Charity and her husband were meeting with an oncologist in the cancer wing of the hospital. They had just received news that confirmed her husband's cancer was incurable and he would die.

As she wept, she heard a noise.

She strained to listen; then she realized what she was hearing—the sound of a bell.

It's tradition for a cancer patient to ring a ceremonial bell when they complete their cancer treatment. The bell symbolizes hope and joy that they've finished.

Charity was losing her husband to cancer, while someone else was beating it. She took a breath. "Stay in your lane, Charity," she told herself.

Charity chose in that moment to be grateful for the time she had with her husband, instead of becoming bitter by drifting into someone else's story.

THE BEST KIND OF CHEERLEADER

Sometimes, cheerleaders get a bad rap.

But one of my best friends is a former high school cheerleader, and she has made me a believer in the power of rooting for others. She is genuinely happy for other people and means it. When I need to be reminded that I can do hard things, I call her. There is a tendency among humans to feel insecure about themselves when another stands out; I have seen the tendency in myself. But I don't see it in my friend. When Rob and I built a house, she was ecstatic for our new adventure. While she herself was squished in a two-bedroom apartment with three kids and a husband, she never made the news of our upgraded living space an opportunity to complain about her small home.

I've asked myself, *how does she feel happy for other people without putting herself down in the process?*

It took me a few years, but I eventually found my answer. She feels genuine happiness for others because she is confident in her own choices. She *stays in her own lane* and lives with intention. She knows that she is supposed to be different. She doesn't compare herself to others, because she knows she's not supposed to be like them. She has found a solution to one of the great thieves of joy and one of the most common causes of dissatisfaction. Comparison.

Why, even as adults, do we struggle so hard with comparison? Shouldn't we have outgrown it already?

Some of us struggle with comparison because we struggle with self-acceptance; we feel threatened when others don't. I have seen it in myself. But everything changes the day we realize we have something unique to offer.

GETTING TO THE ROOT OF COMPARISON

I fell into the trap of comparison at a young age. I remember watching talent shows as a kid, being amazed by the routines and numbers—and feeling upset. I wanted to do what the people on stage did. I wanted to dance like them, play like them, and have an audience applaud me *like them*. I didn't go tell the performers what a good job they did; I didn't want to. I was too upset that I wasn't in their position.

Looking back, I recognize that my insecurities at talent shows weren't about dancing or playing a specific instrument; it was about craving a talent to call my own.

I would love to go sit next to ten-year-old, insecure Julie on the gym floor of Art City Elementary. I would whisper to her, "You *will* stand on a stage one day, and people *will* clap for you."

Feeling insecure is normal, but it might mean that we haven't valued or found what makes us different.

~~~~~~~~~

Before I had kids, I enjoyed a teaching career. When Rob and I found out I was pregnant with our first baby, we made an intentional choice to pause my career. I wanted to stay at home and take care of our child. During this transition, I felt like I was in the middle of an identity crisis.

I switched from an environment full of people and compliments, to an environment that rarely had either. I loved my baby; there was no issue with bonding. However, loving the baby didn't change the loss I felt.

Rob could tell that I was off. I loved being a mom, and I genuinely wanted to be the person at home taking care of my baby. But when I came home from working full time, I gave up a part of my life that brought me a sense of creativity and development. I hadn't found something to replace that part of my life and it was showing.

I was crankier and more judgmental of other people. I hadn't found a way to fulfill my need for creativity as a stay-at-home parent. I was insecure and constantly comparing myself to others, and it resulted in me criticizing the people around me. Putting others down when we feel crappy about ourselves—it's a common, but barf-worthy, behavior.

Rob and I had the same conversation about every other month.

Our exchange went a little like this:

Rob: So . . . what do you want to do for yourself?

Me: What do you mean?

Rob: Well, we've talked about how you want to develop yourself in other ways.

Me: Do you think I'm just sitting home watching Netflix all day?

Rob: No, I know you don't do that.

Me: Are you bothered that I'm not making money?

Rob: No, that's not what I'm saying. I just think you would be happier if you had a space to develop yourself the way you did when you were teaching.

Me: And when would I do that? I'm so tired and overwhelmed. I can't even think about doing something like that.

These conversations often ended in me feeling like Rob didn't think being a stay-at-home parent was important and him feeling like he couldn't say anything about the subject without offending me. The latter was correct.

But he knew me. He knew I could be happier.

DEVELOPING OURSELVES

Slowly, I started crawling out of self-pity and took control of my life. I volunteered in classrooms while a friend watched my kids. I started writing outlines for speeches I wanted to give. I created content to present in front of groups, just like I had done with my curriculum as a second grade teacher.

I began feeling like me again.

When I started speaking and podcasting, I felt something wake up inside. I was learning that I had strengths that were specific to me. I was spending less time comparing myself to others. I learned that I wasn't supposed to be like them. I was meant to be different.

We make space for happiness by developing ourselves; that happiness rubs off on others.

If we don't know how we want to develop ourselves, we can start by trying new things. Elizabeth Gilbert, in her book *Big Magic*, said, "Curiosity only does one thing, and that is to give. And what it gives you are clues on the incredible scavenger hunt of your life."[17]

When we make time to develop ourselves, I've found it's easier to be excited for the successes of others and give genuine compliments. Developing talents can keep us busy and happy, leaving little room to worry about how we measure up to somebody else. When we throw ourselves into our own development, we get a natural boost of energy that comes from becoming the best version of ourselves. As author Chetan Bhagat said, "Be so busy improving yourself that you have no time to criticize others."[18]

Two of my best friends have beautiful voices. In high school, I felt self-conscious to be a part of this trio because I was the only one who didn't sing *above average*. But when I began developing myself in other ways, I no longer felt self-conscious about my voice. Because I knew that I was supposed to be different. Instead of trying to be somebody else, I found myself.

Can you think of one thing you can work on to improve yourself?

OPPORTUNITIES FOR CONNECTION

Finding and developing talents helps us connect with others instead of comparing ourselves to them. We might be tempted to hide our abilities to try to protect others from comparing their weaknesses to our strengths. However, using our strengths to help others enriches relationships and creates unique experiences.

A talented artist in my neighborhood recently offered a free watercolor class to her neighbors. I watched as attendants laughed and made mistakes *together*, exploring a new skill. While the artist could have kept her talent a secret, she chose to use it to create a bonding experience for others.

When we get closer to people and recognize each other's humanity, we are less likely to compare and more likely to connect. If we use our abilities to help other people, we honor the gifts we have been given. In my mind, developing our talents is showing gratitude for them.

GRATITUDE

During a dark chapter of my life, a therapist gave me a simple homework assignment: "Find and acknowledge perfect moments." If a song on the radio came on that I loved, or if I sniffed a familiar smell that brought back memories, my assignment was to recite the words, "This is a perfect moment."

Even though it felt a little robotic, I did my homework. I recognized the perfect moments. While I was scared to say it out loud for fear I would jinx progress, I began to feel sparks of hope just by saying and thinking, "This is a perfect moment." I started contemplating the possibility that I could be happy again.

The more perfect moments I acknowledged, the smaller the gaps between them became. I was looking for reasons to be grateful, and they were everywhere. Gratitude brought me hope.

Almost every religion and school of thought I have studied recognizes gratitude as a fundamental practice to unlock happiness. By choosing to be grateful, we can train our brain to ignore comparing what we *don't* have, to reach for gratitude for what we *do* have. I have learned that "keeping up with the Joneses" isn't nearly as fun as making a party of my own life.

Robert Emmons, professor of psychology, wrote, "Research I've done . . . has suggested that people who have high levels of gratitude have low levels of resentment and envy."[19]

Practicing gratitude can be keeping a gratitude journal where we write down something we are grateful for every day. It can be prayer to a higher power. It can be recognizing a quiet moment.

Gratitude changes our quality of life for the better, and it's an excellent replacement for comparison. When we rid ourselves of comparison, we are making room to see others.

NOT "JUST" ANYTHING

I had the honor of meeting Jon Petz, an inspiring magician and speaker. I listened as he described an experience that changed the way he looked at comparison.

Jon was asked by a friend to perform a magic show for a sick boy at the local hospital. A huge fan of magic, the boy wanted to meet David Copperfield (the magician, not the literary character). As David was unavailable, they called Jon. In his book, *Significance in Simple Moments*, Jon wrote, "How can I possibly compare to David Copperfield?! I'm JUST a magician in Columbus, Ohio. I'm JUST a no-name performer—not a headliner celebrity with his own Las Vegas show. He's a star—I'm JUST Jon Petz! What could I possibly do that would compare to one of the world's greatest magicians?"

Despite his insecurities, Jon agreed to perform a magic show for the sick child.

At the hospital, the boy's tired eyes were filled with wonder as he watched Jon make balls disappear and cards move without a touch. The boy was especially amazed by Jon's final trick. Jon threw a deck of cards high in the air and they all came tumbling down except a seven of hearts (which the boy had privately chosen as "the card") that stuck to the ceiling. Jon left the hospital room feeling inspired and full of love for the sick boy and his family.

The boy passed away the following morning. The family buried the boy with the seven of hearts tucked in his casket. Jon was told, "To them, it symbolized the last happy moment they all had together as a family."

Jon writes, "I was *just* a local magician who didn't even want to go to the hospital that day . . . you are not *just* anything."[20]

Jon didn't need to be David Copperfield to bring hope and wonder to a somber hospital room. He needed to be Jon; a man who was willing to use his talents to bring a smile to the face of a child. And that's exactly what he did. He replaced the comparison eating at him, he got to work, and he saw that boy.

We are exactly who we are supposed to be. All we need to do is be willing to show up and offer what we are to the people who need us.

BE OFFENSIVE

Solely avoiding comparison doesn't get rid of it. We need to replace it with something better. Trying not to compare is defensive; replacing comparison with developing ourselves or expressing gratitude, is offensive. We can find our gifts. We can be thankful for what we have. As we do, we will find it easier to be happy for others. We will *see* people as people, not as competitors.

Last Christmas, my sister shamelessly told me she bought me *the most perfect present ever*. She was feeling no insecurities; she was confident in her talent for personalizing gifts. Her husband told me the same. "Ju, you are going to freak when you see what we got you for Christmas!" Their enthusiasm made me laugh and I felt loved, knowing they had put thought into the gift they chose. On Christmas morning, I opened the long-awaited present. The self-assured couple was right; they nailed it.

The gift was a wooden plaque, inscribed with a quote that puts comparison in its place; a quote by Theodore Roosevelt.

> It is not the critic who counts; not the man who points out how the strong man stumbles, or where the doer of deeds could have done them better. The credit belongs to the man who is actually in the arena, whose face is marred by dust and sweat and blood;

who strives valiantly; who errs, who comes short again and again, because there is no effort without error and shortcoming; but who does actually strive to do the deeds; who knows great enthusiasms, the great devotions; who spends himself in a worthy cause; who at the best knows in the end the triumph of high achievement, and who at the worst, if he fails, at least fails while daring greatly, so that his place shall never be with those cold and timid souls who neither know victory nor defeat.[21]

These words hang over my desk where I create. They watch me and keep me in check. We can't let comparison destroy us; we need that energy to pursue our own dreams. Then we can encourage others to do the same; that's *seeing* them.

We all feel insecure sometimes. We might be tempted to judge others for being brave, for doing things we don't have the guts to do. We might even feel threatened by their accomplishments. But we have our own talents to develop; our song to sing.

When we shed comparison from our mindset, we are set up to help others succeed. Instead of seeing people for what they *can't* do, we can give them confidence in what they *can* do. Someone who doesn't compare themselves to others inspires people to shine in their own light.

The Bottom Line

Comparison keeps us from seeing others with compassion and connecting with them. We avoid the crippling effects of comparison by practicing gratitude and developing our own gifts. By discarding comparison, we are ready to help others do the same.

Part Three

Who They Need

Chapter 7

Leaders Who Shine

When you stop expecting people to be perfect,
you can like them for who they are.[22]

—Donald Miller

In elementary school, Clint couldn't keep still. He dealt with his constant energy by tapping. As you can imagine, his tapping did not go unnoticed. He drove teachers crazy and he was made fun of by classmates. Nicknames like "twitcher," "tapper," and "twitch" made him feel small. But he couldn't stop tapping.

In fifth grade, Clint's teacher, Mr. Jensen, asked Clint to stay after class. Preparing himself for another visit to the principal's office, Clint stayed and waited for his recompense.

Mr. Jensen looked at Clint from across the desk, and said, "I've noticed you Clint. I've noticed you tapping." He asked Clint to tap both hands at the same time, but at different speeds. Clint did it. "I knew it! I knew it!" Mr. Jensen exclaimed. He looked at Clint and said the sentence that changed Clint's life forever. "You are not a problem. Clint, I think you are a drummer."

He opened his desk drawer and pulled out a pair of brand-new drumsticks. He told Clint to keep them in his hands and see what happened.

Fast forward a few years.

Clint Pulver has been a professional drummer for over twenty years. He's played with top headlining fellow musicians in the Kodak Theater in Hollywood. In 2010, he founded and directed the *Green Man Group*. He performed on *America's Got Talent*. He went on to direct the Drumline for the NBA's Utah Jazz until 2015.

Now Clint spends his life traveling all over the world, training leaders to inspire; he tells them about Mr. Jensen.[23]

It made all the difference to have a mentor who invested in Clint's potential.

THE CLASSROOM

My father was diagnosed with bipolar disorder when I was three years old. The diagnosis came at a time when there wasn't much awareness of mental illness. We experienced happy times and hard times as a family. As a child, I dealt with fear, confusion, and felt ultimately responsible for my parents' happiness.

I didn't know how to process my emotions as a kid. In my young mind, I would be ungrateful to express disappointment, anger, or hurt when my family was already struggling. I didn't want to be a reason for more pain in our home. From a young age, I committed myself to making others happy. I pushed my painful feelings deep down inside, where I thought they disappeared. But I was wrong.

The symptoms started when I was twenty-one years old. Nightmares, flashbacks, crippling anxiety, and depression. Therapists said it looked a lot like PTSD. But what triggered it?

A toxic mentor.

I was student teaching through a national program, thousands of miles away from my university. The teacher who was assigned to mentor me didn't get the memo that I was coming. She seemed to dislike me from the start. She glared at me while I taught, criticized my compassion for the students, and laughed at my ideas. Looking back, I can see it wasn't a safe work environment. That kind of environment stunts growth and instills fear.

I thought I could please my mentor by working harder than ever. Not so. Five exhausting weeks later, I was in a faculty bathroom stall, stifling back my first panic attack and the vomit that was trying to come up my throat.

That was the beginning of the mental breakdown that followed.

I couldn't sleep, eat, or be alone; both my body and mind were in an unrelenting state of fear. I called an advisor I knew I could trust: Kerri, a previous instructor from my university. Hearing my sobs through the phone, she asked, "What *happened to you* out there?" I did my best to convey an accurate picture of the last five weeks. After communicating with the Education Department, she advised me to discontinue student teaching and come home. She promised to help me get back on my feet. I was on a plane within days.

The first day I walked back into a classroom, I only made it two hours.

Through tears, I apologized to my new mentor teacher, told her I couldn't do it and left the school. I was sure I would never step into a school as a teacher again. My confidence in my ability to lead a classroom was shattered.

I listened to a voicemail from Kerri later that day. My new mentor teacher had called her and told her about my swift exit. The voice message was free of shame and disappointment; she told me we would try again, one hour at a time if necessary.

Little by little, I crawled my way back. After my first teaching observation, Kerri held my hand and cried with me. She gave me my observation sheet to look at later. Right now, she told me, we needed to talk about what was most important: me and my mental health.

LEADERS WHO CARE

Clint needed Mr. Jensen to bring awareness to his gift. He needed Mr. Jensen to show him that his tapping wasn't a problem, it was a solution. Clint learned that he didn't have to run from who he was; engaging in his natural ability gave him confidence and purpose. The gift of two drumsticks changed his life forever.

Just like Clint needed a mentor who saw his tapping as a gift, I needed a mentor like Kerri.

I needed a mentor to believe in me when my confidence was crumbling. I needed someone who could provide encouragement and safety; to help me rebuild my skill set. While she had a full schedule, she made time for me. She reminded me of who I could become.

I often wonder what would have happened to me, had Kerri not been so patient with me. It's likely I never would have returned to the classroom, never would have graduated college, and I never would have become a teacher. Because of her willingness to invest in me, I did all of those things.

After graduating college, I interviewed for and was offered two teaching positions. I was torn. While one position was more what I had pictured for my teaching career, the principal who interviewed me at the other school exuded support. Those in my hiring interview won me over. They saw me as a great fit to their team, and their vision empowered me to prove them right. Teaching with people who built me up was one of the best decisions I ever made.

Are we providing this kind of connection and safety as leaders? Are we seeing those we guide as human beings with great potential? When we build the people we lead, we give them a reason to prove us right. As author Simon Sinek wrote, "A boss has the title, a leader has the people."

As we look at our circle of influence, we can ask ourselves if we are leading with compassion and connection. Are we going to bat for those who look up to us most? Do we look them in the eyes when we talk to them? Are we invested in them?

People need positive leaders who believe in their gifts. We can be that person. We can create an environment where people feel safe enough to innovate, take risks, and make mistakes.

We can learn to shine as leaders when we consider the patience we strive to have with kids. Adults are just big kids after all.

THE UNCONDITIONAL LOVE
OF POTTY TRAINING

Leading with unconditional love reminds me of potty training. I think it's a good example of leading with love, no matter how *crappy* someone's choices are.

Out of respect for my children who will one day be teenagers, and who might care what people think (although I'm working on a special antidotal serum for that), I regretfully refrain from too many specifics in this section. Sammy and Lydee, just know Mama loves you and never, ever wants to potty train you again.

Gear up, it's about to get graphic.

When I potty trained my kids, I gave them positive feedback long before they successfully got their business *in* the toilet bowl. Rob and I enthusiastically cheered them on for simply sitting *on* the toilet. We didn't wait until they had done the precise deed we were hoping for. We congratulated them on progress, progress that would lead them to the outcome we wanted. In the beginning, we could have said, "Sitting *on* the potty isn't enough. You need to get something *in* the potty, then we'll celebrate." No, we got them jazzed about sitting *on* the toilet long before verbalizing the expectation that they produce something *in* it.

I have to exercise patience *daily* during potty training, because giving unconditional love while cleaning out underwear in the toilet is truly a test of patience. It takes intentional focus and self-control. We can give the people we lead that same intense, unconditional love I strive to give my toddlers. We can be happy that they show up and that they are still trying. Especially when situations are *crappy*, we can dig in deep and find the will to be compassionate.

We can celebrate the good in those who look to us for support. While we don't reward them with shiny stickers (the way I do with my kids when they try to go "potty"), sincere smiles and direct eye contact go a long way.

As my wise Grandmother once advised me about keeping a husband happy, "Let him hear you praise him and he will stand two inches taller." By emphasizing strengths, we can create an environment where people love to be.

The Bottom Line

We can be a Kerri or a Mr. Jensen. We can lead the people we mentor with greater compassion, connect with them, and highlight the gifts they have to offer. People are more likely to meet and even exceed our expectations when they know we have their back.

Chapter 8

What Makes Us Powerful

Maybe being different isn't so bad after all.

—"Broccolipunzle: A Fractured Fairytale"

I have only been asked out by a blow-up toy *once*.

As a sophomore in college, I woke up to a life-size, inflatable Leprechaun standing in my living room, with a note taped to his chest. The note was from a boy in apartment twenty, asking me on a date. This guy was wacky from the start.

He took me to a comedy show and after, we picked up some frozen yogurt. As we walked back to our apartment building, he said, "Tell me a story." Still giggly from the comedy show, I invented a bizarre fairytale off the top of my head. "Once upon a time, there was a princess. But she wasn't an ordinary princess; this princess was born with broccoli for hair."

When I finished the story, my date applauded with enthusiasm. I think he genuinely liked it; I also think he was trying to get a second date. His praise convinced me to submit the story for my Children's Literature class project. I typed it up just hours before the assignment was due and copied and pasted a clipart leaf that would have to pass for broccoli. I recognize now that the leaf looked a lot more like marijuana than broccoli. I entitled the story, *Broccolipunzle: A Fractured Fairy Tale.*

I need to tell you more about this untraditional princess. Her story serves as an omen for things to come.

Broccolipunzle hates having broccoli for hair. She has to trim the moldy ends, wash it, and sleep in the fridge once a week to keep it from wilting. She also has to deal with unwanted attention from others.

One night, as she is complaining about her hair, her fairy godmother appears. Godmother has come to rid Broccolipunzle of her broccoli hair and promises to replace it with shiny locks. All she requires is that the princess take twenty-four hours to think about her decision. Does she truly want to be rid of her broccoli hair forever?

The next day, Broccolipunzle comes across a hungry man, slumped on the side of the road. In a spirit of true generosity, she cuts off some of her broccoli hair and shares it with him. She loves the way it feels to give to someone. All through the village, she offers her healthy florets to the villagers. They love their princess for her generous spirit. In the end, Broccolipunzle tells the fairy godmother she wants to keep her hair. She no longer despises sleeping in the refrigerator once a week or trimming the moldy ends. She has learned to love her hair because of the opportunity it gives her to help others. Her trial has taken on new meaning.

I got an A- on the project. I suspect it was the marijuana leaf clipart that docked my grade.

And the wacky boy? I married him the following year.

Nine years later, on my twenty-seventh birthday, Rob gave me a special present; a hardback copy of my story. *Broccolipunzle: A Fractured Fairytale,* was complete with illustrations done by a friend. Rob thought it needed to be shared. The story began circulating among family and friends.

After reading my book to her kids, my sister called on the phone and said, "Julie, I was reading this book out loud and I started crying. This isn't just a children's book, this is a book for everybody. Julie, this is a book about spiritual gifts." Shivers went down my spine. The truth in her words overwhelmed me.

I thought about Broccolipunzle's generosity when she cut off her hair to feed a stranger. Generosity was an innate gift she already possessed. When she combined her generosity with an unexpected, and even painful, part of her life (having broccoli for hair) she became more than a princess; she became a hero.

I started talking to kids, to adults, to anyone who would listen. Teaching each and every one of them—what makes you *different* makes you *powerful*. I have now used the message of *Broccolipunzle* to speak to thousands of people about self-acceptance and innate talents. Everyone has something to share, a superpower they can use to *see* others.

IDENTIFYING A SUPERPOWER

My definition of a *gift* is a talent that comes naturally. A *superpower* is made when we combine that gift with our transformative life experiences.

What is *my* superpower to give? What gift can I combine with my plot twist? I've been people-crazy for as long as I can remember. I love being around other people, connecting with them, and learning their stories. From a young age, making friends came easily to me; that is one of my gifts.

My broccoli hair is easy to identify. I graduated college, I married a good guy, and that's when the plot twist came. Depression and anxiety was the broccoli hair, the life experience that I spent years wishing a fairy godmother would take away. Once I stopped running from my challenge, accepted it, and found healing, my experiences gave me insight into how to help others. Combining my insight into mental health (broccoli hair) and my ability to connect with others (innate gift) has resulted in one of my greatest treasures and superpowers, the *I See You* mission. I work everyday to strengthen my superpower; to *see* people better.

Not long ago, I came to a realization. I confided in my friend, "*Broccolipunzle* isn't a story about a princess with broccoli for hair. This is a story about me! This is my story." Like only a good friend can, she surprised me with, "You really just figured that out?"

Could *Broccolipunzle* be about you too?

FINDING OUR GIFTS

While we can certainly try to improve skills that don't come easily to us, we each have innate talents waiting to be polished, and we might get more bang for our buck when we hone in on what we are naturally good at. Our gifts are uniquely ours to share with the world.

Close your eyes and picture something you are good at. Something you've always had a knack for, since the day you were born.

Are you amazing with kids?

Do you catch on to concepts quickly?

Do you connect with others easily?

Are you articulate?

Are you a good listener?

What gifts are yours?

A SPECIAL PILLOW

When my sister, Amy, underwent cancer treatments during her pregnancy, many people rallied around her, supporting her by offering the talents they had to share. One of the most meaningful gifts she received was from a woman in Southern California who learned about the situation and wanted to do something to help. An accomplished seamstress, she put her skills to work and sewed a special pillow for my sister.

After Amy's son was born, she immediately underwent a second mastectomy. Recovery was challenging and her chest was sensitive. Amy had agonized over what she could do to connect with her baby. She wanted so badly to hold him close, to comfort him. A package from Southern California arrived in the mail, just in time. The pillow was specially made to strap around her body in such a way that she could hold the baby close to her face, without feeling pain from the pressure of the baby on her chest. It was a powerful offering and will never be forgotten.

The woman who served my sister is an example of using a unique talent to bring relief to a situation. It was sweet to learn that this humble seamstress also happens to be the mother-in-law of Tim Ballard, who wrote the foreword to this book.

THE 4:1 RATIO

Our gifts will not always be appreciated.

I had a sad neighbor. I often saw her in the afternoon as she walked to the mailbox, still wearing her pajamas, then returned to her house. The curtains were always closed. She looked unhappy. Anxious to put my gift of making friends to use, I looked for ways to interact with her. Often, I crossed the street when I saw her getting her mail and struck up a conversation. We talked about our kids, our pets, and our jobs. I thought our relationship was becoming solid and I enjoyed learning from her perspective.

One day, a friend from the other side of the neighborhood was chatting with me in my kitchen. She was close to the neighbor I was befriending. She confided that my neighbor had said she didn't like me. She found my questions nosy.

We all have moments when a negative experience makes us question our abilities.

I felt sick. I thought conversing with my neighbor was benefiting her, but she felt uncomfortable with my approach. I asked myself, "Do I overwhelm people?" Instead of helping my neighbor, I had annoyed her. I liked people; I certainly didn't want to annoy them.

It's important to evaluate the criticism we are given—is there truth in it, and if so, how can we improve? Considering the feedback I was given, I decided I wanted to change.

I thought of my friends who are more reserved than me, and I used their disposition as a model to emulate. For the next few days, I spoke less. I didn't talk to strangers in line at the post office. I didn't ask the cashier at the store if they liked their job.

How did I feel after a few days of the *new me*? Awful. I felt smaller than I did the day I was told my neighbor called me *nosy*. Stifling who I was felt worse than the criticism.

Interestingly enough, within that same week, I had four different people in my neighborhood express gratitude for my outgoing nature. "I am so grateful that you introduced yourself;" "I was so scared when I moved here, you were the first person to talk to me;" "You made me feel like things might be okay because I had a friend."

If you could see me now, I would hold up one hand with four fingers in the air. The other hand would be up as well, with one single finger raised. I get to choose which hand to put in front of my face. I can center my attention on the hand with four fingers up or the hand that has one. Which do I choose to look at? I can choose to focus on the feedback of *one person* who thought my talent was annoying. Or, I can choose to concentrate on the feedback I received from *four sources* who told me my talent helped them.

I choose to focus on the four fingers; the four people I helped. I choose to be *me*.

To be the powerful beings we were born to be, we must always stay *us*. Our goal should be to become the best version of *us*.

Seeing people by using our talents requires vulnerability, but the payoff is worth it. Knowing that we are changing and saving lives by using our gifts to spur connection is a rich, honest life.

BROCCOLI FOR HAIR

Most of us want to help other people—that's probably why we are reading this book. We might have a vision for exactly *how* we will make the world a better place. Maybe we want to make a lot of money so we can bring financial relief to the poor. Maybe we want to be the party house, where our teenagers choose to bring their friends.

But, what if we lose our job and can barely provide for our own family? What if our teenager hates being home, despite our best efforts to connect with them? Amidst these setbacks, we have the opportunity to make the world a better place with *the hand we are dealt*.

John Lennon sang, "Life is what happens when you are busy making other plans."[24] We each have our own plot twists, disappointments, and detours; life circumstances that were never part of our plan.

As we look at our life with an eye of curiosity, we can find our own broccoli hair. If we let them, life's surprises can be opportunities to connect with others. We don't always get to choose how our life unfolds, but we do get to choose what we do with it.

PUTTING A SUPERPOWER TO USE

By honoring our experiences *and* talents we can craft a superpower that rescues others.

I have a twelve-year-old niece named Maren whose natural gift is noticing others. She enjoys picking out thoughtful gifts for family, making friends with those left out, and entertaining small children without being asked. Basically, she takes after her mom, my big sister, Jenny, whose heart knows no bounds.

Maren also has a rare connective tissue disorder called Loeys-Dietz Syndrome (LDS). Her childhood has been different than her siblings and friends. She can't participate in contact sports or strenuous exercise; pushing herself too hard could lead to serious complications. She can't wear the cute shoes most girls her age are wearing. If she does, she struggles with foot pain and even sprains. Scoliosis and loose joints make backpacks painful to wear. A friend of hers with the same condition recently passed away, leaving Maren asking, "Will the same thing happen to me?"

I have watched Maren combine her awareness of others (her gift) with her disorder (her broccoli hair), resulting in a mesmerizing superpower. To illustrate, I'll share a portion of an essay she recently wrote for a school assignment.

> If I were a superhero, I would have the power to heal the sick and injured. . . . I would go to the hospital every week and heal everyone I could. . . . I love my powers so much but at the same time I hate them, because sometimes I can't always save everyone because there's only one of me and millions of them. . . . I'm Miracle Girl and I hope I will always do good for this world and everyone in it. I want to help others live up to their full potential. In my heart I will always think of myself as Miracle Girl.[25]

Maren makes presents and cards to deliver to patients in the hospital. Maren's superpower is empathy in action. She *is* Miracle Girl to me.

What our superpowers have in common is they are needed. We don't need to talk in front of large groups the way I like to, or hand out presents in hospitals like Maren does. There are countless ways to share light, and being true to who *we* are is just what the world needs.

The Bottom Line

When we combine our transformative life experiences with our talents, we develop our own superpowers that help us *see* others.

Chapter 9

The Art of Authenticity

We are constantly invited to be what we are.[26]

—Henry David Thoreau

I've been complimented in the past for the way I've handled my mental struggles. I have mixed feelings about some of the compliments I received. One person told me, "I am amazed by your strength; I wish my sister could be more like you. You struggle with depression but I would have no idea because you always act so happy!"

While I wholeheartedly agree with finding joy in our obstacles, I don't love the idea of complimenting someone because they don't show they are hurting. Are we teaching each other that it's a sign of strength to pretend we are okay when we are not?

I have spent the last decade trying to exercise a positive outlook *and* practice raw authenticity; an authenticity that ain't always positive.

How can we see others if we aren't willing to be seen ourselves?

AN OPPORTUNITY TO BE AUTHENTIC

Rob and I wanted kids. Even before we were *trying* to have kids, I always thought I was pregnant. If I felt the slightest hint of nausea, I raced to the dollar store to buy a pregnancy test. I cried when it came back negative. Rob was perplexed by my emotional outbursts; we had agreed to wait until I finished my college degree. Logically, I *did* want to wait until I finished school to have a child. Emotionally, I was elated at the idea of becoming pregnant before then.

When we did start trying for a baby, each unsuccessful month was devastating. Once you know you want babies, it feels like an *eternity*, no matter how long you have to wait. At least it did for me. We had been trying for a baby for eight months when we moved out of state. We would only be gone four months; my dad reassured me that I would be pregnant by the time we got back.

I wasn't.

But my mom birthed seven children in her lifetime and my sisters (including my brothers' wives) were all poppin' out babies like popcorn. My family knows how to reproduce. Why wasn't I able to?

We did testing. You know it's bad when they refuse to give you results over the phone. The doctor said both Rob and I had infertility problems. I was floored.

For the next few years, we became well acquainted with fertility drugs and procedures. I still laugh when I think of Rob's first job interview, post grad-school. The interviewer asked about the limp in his walk. Without missing a beat, my husband confidently responded, "Oh, I just had surgery so we can have kids." My husband has never lacked honesty. He got the job.

Doctors eventually decided that our only shot at having biological children was through In Vitro Fertilization (IVF). It was the most invasive fertility procedure available; it was also expensive and that meant more waiting.

I had a radar for pregnant women—they were EVERYWHERE. Everyone seemed to be having babies. And church sermons about the importance of family? Yeah, those were just torturous.

Again and again, I had to choose how to respond to the common greeting, *how are you?* Being the open book that I am, I chose to stay authentic to my nature. When I felt happy, I said so. When I was sad that I didn't have a baby on my hip, I said that too.

Our burdens can feel lighter when we share our feelings with friends we trust, and sometimes, strangers who cross our paths at pivotal moments. While some things are necessary to keep private,

I've found that it's important to remain authentic through our experiences, especially the tough ones. The more we process our negative feelings, the more we make room for positive ones. Also, when we are honest with ourselves and others, we provide opportunities for others to be honest with us.

LETTING PEOPLE SEE US

Remember those sisters, the popcorn makers who were popping out all the babies? I cried to them a lot. They understood. I knew I wasn't alone.

One evening I texted one of my popcorn makers, telling her *I just need someone out there to know that while most of the time I am happy, tonight I am so heartbroken and all I want is a baby.* She responded with compassion and saw me perfectly, like she always does.

As I opened up to my sisters and friends about my infertility, they in turn, became more open with me about their own struggles. Their vulnerability helped me feel comfortable sharing my life with them. It didn't matter whether the person sitting with me had struggled with infertility or not; they loved me and trusted me with their own pain. Those are the only qualifications required to cry with me.

During our experiences with infertility, our friends hosted a 5K at a nearby park to raise money for their own In Vitro Fertilization (IVF) procedure. After the race, the husband stood in front of the crowd and shared personal feelings about their infertility journey. I was familiar with the heartache he described. I walked out of the crowd crying.

I sat next to a nearby creek where I could sob my face off.

I felt a hand on my shoulder; two women had followed me from the race. Without hesitation, they threw their arms around me. They held me. So. Tight. These women, who had no experience with infertility of their own and multiple kids to show for it, sat and talked with me. They asked about my experience. They asked me what it felt like to wait and Wait and WAIT. They wanted to "get it." They *saw me.* They chose to be vulnerable and get in the real stuff with me. Their example of being authentic with me gave me permission to be authentic in return.

Being authentic is being willing to say, "I don't know what you are going through, but you are a human being and that means you are worthy of my time." It is not required—or possible—to understand every situation.

One year during our infertility saga, I received a package just before Mother's Day. My sister, Christy, organized members on both sides of my family to shower me with love. The package was filled with personal notes outlining my best qualities, and messages of gratitude for how I mothered my nieces and nephews. Christy also included a necklace with "eventually" inscribed on it. After that, Rob and I referred to our long-awaited day of having a baby as our "eventually day" and continued to hope for it.

During my IVF procedure, Christy also helped me refinish a dresser to get my mind off it. Another sister came and did a puzzle with me while I had to lie flat on my back for two days, in hopes the pregnancy would take. That little apartment was filled with light, becoming brighter and brighter with each person who visited me.

We got the news at the top of a mountain in Idaho, straddling the four-wheeler we drove to find cell phone service. When my doctor told us that I was pregnant, Rob and I both reacted in a moment of complete authenticity. I cried. Rob kissed me and said, "You look so hot pregnant."

Five years after getting married, we finally had a fresh newborn to snuggle. We got our Sam. The IVF treatment gave us our son.

Fertility doctors had given us a one-in-a-million chance of getting pregnant on our own.

On Christmas Eve, ten months after Sam was born, we beat those odds. I found out with *a dollar store pregnancy test* in my own tiny bathroom. A second baby was on her way.

I cried in sheer gratitude the day we found out. The next day, I cried in sheer terror; I was afraid that I couldn't raise two children, eighteen months apart. Authenticity means accepting *all* the feelings.

We are grateful to be raising two miracles. Because Rob and I were willing to be seen in our struggle, we were taught by example how to *see* someone who is hurting.

AUTHENTICITY GETS US THROUGH

It's easy to be authentic about our story of struggle after the struggle is gone. It's a lot harder to be authentic in the middle of our story when nothing is making sense.

We all know people who haven't arrived at their *eventually* day. We don't know why. They haven't been able to find the job, the cure, or the spouse they've been hoping for. It isn't fair. These people can teach us about living an authentic life, as they wait for their eventually day and allow us to see them as they are. When someone is waiting for *their* eventually day, they need the hope that compassion and connection offer. We can offer just that by being relatable and unashamed of our own unpredictable life.

SOMEONE TO RELATE TO

Do we ever wish we were the Pinterest version of ourselves? A person who has it all together, all the time? A person who has no concerns, no heartbreaks, no insecurities, and no shame triggers?

I've never met someone like that. Have you?

We don't need to try to fit a certain mold. The more authentic we are, the more we stop wasting our energy on trying to be something else, and we have the reserves needed to focus on other people.

We are who we are for a reason. We have experienced our experiences for a reason. Sharing our stories authentically will remind others that *they are not alone.*

SOLVING OUR PROBLEMS

What if we were sincerely authentic about our challenges and allowed others to do the same?

What if we said to our spouse, "Hey, I am struggling to stay sober, can we go for a hike to help ground me?" Or "I feel taken advantage of at work. Can I vent to you?" We have to get authentic about our problems and become *transparent*, if we are to ever find healing.

When we recognize our weaknesses, we'll be happier, we'll be more honest, and when the people around us notice—they just might follow suit. We can let ourselves be seen in our problems. We can look around and see people in theirs. Together, we can solve any problem.

The Bottom Line

Being authentic means allowing ourselves to be seen in our joys *and* our struggles. It takes courage and humility. Practicing authenticity is a choice that gives others permission to be authentic in return, making it easier to *see* them and their needs.

Chapter 10

We Are The Light

*Happiness can be found in the darkest of times,
if only we remember to turn on the light.*[27]

—Albus Dumbledore in *Harry Potter
and the Prisoner of Azkaban*

I am no science prodigy.

I was the girl in the back of science class, staring intently at the clock, begging the hands to rotate faster. When people start geeking out over science, or worse, *technology*, I feel my eyes begin to roll in the back of my head out of sheer exhaustion.

I didn't stand in that line in heaven.

However, the scientific concept of light became important to me when depression and anxiety made life feel dark. I look at light differently now.

Christmas lights.

Candles.

The *sun*.

I love light.

The cool thing about light is this: *we cannot see color without light.* We see color when the reflection of light bounces off an object and enters our cornea. For example, when we see a yellow banana, what we are actually seeing is the reflection of light bouncing off the banana and coming back through our cornea which results in the color yellow.

Light creates color. The symbolic implication this piece of information provides makes me want to geek out over science; it's that cool.

Tim Ballard helped me see light in a whole new way.

THE POWER OF LIGHT

I wanted Tim, the founder of Operation Underground Railroad, or O.U.R. to write the foreword of this book for a reason. Tim is a former homeland security operative who decided to leave his government job to start a nonprofit organization to rescue children from sex trafficking. There are few jobs more important than Tim's.

Throughout his years of service, Tim has gone undercover as someone seeking to buy children for sex. As you can imagine, he has interacted with some of the darkest human beings on the planet. To keep his cover, Tim befriends them.

Tim has seen darkness. This is why he is such an advocate of finding light.

I have listened to Tim give several public addresses on the subject of finding light. As someone who is fascinated with the idea of light, in both a literal and figurative sense, I love conversations about it. Tim often shares the story of two kids he met at a staged orphanage in Haiti; these kids can teach us about light.

During this mission, Tim held a three-year-old boy who he agreed to "buy." He walked around the orphanage with the child in his arms, scouting out the location. He noticed a shadow. A terrified little girl was following close behind. Her name was Coline. Not wanting to draw attention to himself, Tim gave Coline a candy bar and told her to go back to the other kids. Coline did something Tim had never seen a child do before. She took the candy bar, broke it in half, and gave half of the chocolate to the boy in Tim's arms. In that moment, Tim suspected the truth that was in front of him—this boy and Coline were brother and sister. He assumed that Coline was following him because she knew he might take her little brother away, the way she had watched so many other children be taken by white men who came to buy them.

Why would this little girl, who was near starvation, give her brother the chocolate? Tim explains that she was hanging on to the light inside her. Amidst the horrific things going on around her, she maintained her light. What is that light? It is the choice to care for another. We keep and grow the light within us when we reach out and save someone. Light is compassion and light is love.

Tim says, "There is one thing I know for certain; light and darkness can never share the same place at the same time. The key is knowing how to keep the lights on inside, no matter how dark it is outside." This little girl kept the lights on inside by looking outside of herself and doing what she could. She couldn't save her brother from this "orphanage," and she couldn't save him from being sold; but she could give him half her chocolate bar.

After leaving the orphanage that day, Tim couldn't stop thinking about the brother and sister. Although he had trained himself to emotionally disconnect as a survival tactic, this time he couldn't detach.

After years of waiting for the adoption to finalize, Tim and his wife, Kathryn, brought these two Haitian orphans home to live with them; they now live in the United States and their last name is Ballard.

Light overcomes darkness. We all make mistakes. We each have the power to reject darkness and replace it with light.

KEEPING THE LIGHTS ON

If we want to see people with clarity, to connect and have compassion on them, we need to feed the light within us. It's nearly impossible to see people if the lights are out.

Sometimes darkness comes into our lives through no fault of our own. Chemical imbalances and traumatic experiences can make it especially difficult to feel the light. I am grateful for medication, therapy, and all resources dedicated to helping those of us affected in this way.

Darkness can also come from bad decisions.

It can also come from being self-absorbed with either pride or self-loathing; both of which cause us to focus inward. While self-care and reflection are imperative to living a balanced life, thinking too much about ourselves can cause the light to dim.

Getting lost in our own problems can make it hard to recognize that we aren't alone. Looking outward helps us keep perspective. When we focus *only* inward, it's hard to notice the people right in front of our eyes who need us. Or if we do notice them, we might not have the emotional energy to reach out. Making peace with ourselves clears space for us to help others.

I love the analogy of a handheld mirror and how it relates to seeing outside ourselves. When we hold a mirror close to our face, we can't see anything past it. We can't see if there is a person standing behind the mirror; all we see is our own face. It isn't until we put the mirror down that we are able to see other people. To be able to say "I see you" to someone and mean it, we can't be staring at ourselves in a mirror, either analyzing our imperfections or amplifying our accomplishments.

When we look outside ourselves for opportunities to save the people around us, our light becomes more powerful. And—our light is contagious.

My husband and I lived apart for five weeks while he completed an internship. One evening, I was feeling dark. I called him and expressed my feelings. He asked me if he could sing me a song on the guitar to help bring me peace. I cried on the bed as Rob played his guitar and sang to me from 1,400 miles away. His light traveled across multiple states and got me through a hard night. It was a ray of hope that transcended the dark.

LIGHT IS THERE WHEN YOU NEED IT

As I am writing this, people all over the globe are physically isolating due to the Coronavirus pandemic. Many don't leave their homes, and if they do, it's only for essential purposes, like grocery shopping or picking up a prescription. It is interesting to observe human behavior during this unusual time of social distancing. Whether it's watching people at Wal-Mart (staying the mandated six feet away from others) or scrolling through my social media newsfeed, I see a wide spectrum of reactions.

Some people are scared. Some people are overwhelmed. Some people turn on each other under the stress of uncertainty. Mostly, I have seen light. I have seen light in the Costco employee telling us jokes while we stand in line, awaiting our one allotted package of toilet paper. I have seen light in the text messages that read, "Does your family have everything you need?" or "I'm headed to the store, can I get you anything?" I have seen light in the smiles of people all around me, as they walk on the other side of the sidewalk, out of respect for our human race and the pandemic we currently face.

I have watched people in decorated cars parade through our neighborhood while honking their horn and shaking their "Happy Birthday" signs. They came for a thirteen-year-old boy who couldn't have a party with friends on his special day.

I have seen inspirational quotes written in sidewalk chalk during our community's spontaneous *Chalk the Walk* event. Our family won the "Best Christmas at Easter Award" for our depiction of Whoville, the Grinch, and his trustee dog, Max.

That's a made-up award if I ever saw one.

Rob and I loved the award as much as our kids did. The person who left it found a way to connect; to show my family that our messy chalk illustrations had been noticed. It doesn't matter how old we are, we all want to be noticed by someone.

I have seen people gravitating towards connection. I have seen light in people; so bright that it shines from six feet away.

In 1948, a C. S. Lewis essay was published entitled "On Living on an Atomic Age." His words seem to relate to our current world situation, as we face our own uncertain future. He wrote,

> This is the first point to be made: and the first action to be taken is to pull ourselves together. If we are all going to be destroyed by an atomic bomb, let that bomb when it comes find us doing sensible and human things — praying, working, teaching, reading, listening to music, bathing the children, playing tennis, chatting to our friends over a pint and a game of darts — not huddled together like

frightened sheep and thinking about bombs. They may break our bodies . . . but they need not dominate our minds.[28]

C. S. Lewis had it right. We feel hope when we refuse to let fear "dominate our minds." We add light to a situation when we serve our fellow citizens, even if we can't be on the same side of the aisle. When obstacles try to block us from each other, we can find creative ways to connect with each other.

I have a sister who might be more extroverted than I am. You'll hear her before you see her. In light of the social distancing we have experienced during the Coronavirus pandemic, she sent me a meme that said, "Introverts, put down your books and check on your extroverted friends. We are not okay." I laughed. We extroverts *are* okay when we find creative ways to connect. We have to find a way to share our light, no matter what kind of "vert" we are.

Light is service. Service is light. We can share our candy bar. We can play our song. We can buy our neighbor some extra toilet paper. We can do *something*.

Our light is like a muscle; the more we use it, the stronger it gets. If we share our light with other people, it's unlikely we'll ever lose it. We will be happier too. Higher quality of life and saving lives; light is a win.

The Bottom Line

We each have light inside us and service makes it grow. Light helps us see people with compassion, giving us a greater ability to connect with them. When we put down the mirror, we will see who needs us today.

Part Four

Tools to See

Chapter 11

Finding Funny

*Do you live each day as if it's your first or your last?
Either way, you should probably have a diaper on.*[29]

—Ellen DeGeneres

My sister, Amy, is one of the most funny and present people I know.

Amy was caring for her five (now six) rambunctious kids, when between diaper changes and imagination games, she looked in the mirror to see something no human should *ever* see.

Poop.

In her hair.

I only put this story in the book because I think the humor outweighs the urge I have to gag while writing about it; perhaps you have the same urge reading about it.

Amy didn't know what to do. In a panic, she grabbed the phone and called a friend who lived just up the street. "I don't know how to say this," she half laughed/half cried, "I have poop in my hair! Can you come help me?" Her friend, equally amused and concerned, rushed to the house, took the baby off my sister's hip, and Amy ran to the shower to clean her body inside out. Oh, and to wash her hair. I see you, Amy; and that is disgusting.

This story is funny to me, and it is to Amy, too, now that it's over. Her friend *saw* her in a way that deserves a big, Oreo milkshake. Amy did her part by being authentic and willing to be seen; she also knew the exact person who could jump into this hilarious, disgusting situation with her. That says something about her friend. Finding humor in life can be a powerful way to connect and have compassion on others and ourselves.

What a good benchmark to have for ourselves! Are we the person someone would call if they were in this situation? I call this the *Poop in the Hair Standard*. We are real enough that someone would call us and tell us that they have poop in their hair, knowing that we would rescue them in the moment, and laugh about it with us later.

Amy deserves credit too. She made the phone call. Even during a crisis, my sister has the unique ability to maintain a sense of humor that makes me wet my pants.

FUNNY GETS PEOPLE THROUGH

Amidst the beginning of my mental health journey, Amy and I came up with a funny name for the version of me that was full of anxiety and spiraling in and out of panic attacks. Like an evil twin. We named her Delilah.

Not like Samson and Delilah from the Bible. Like Delilah, the song, which introduced and concluded the talk radio show hosted by Delilah. Her name was sung in a serious and dramatic way, and that's how Amy and I said it.

My big sister found me in the middle of more than one panic attack. She put her arms around my shoulders, pulled me in close, and held me. "Delilah's back," I would cry. She nodded; she had become acquainted with Delilah. Other times, I proclaimed to Amy, "Delilah is gone!" We laughed and we lived in that moment of hope.

Delilah was truly the worst, but her name still makes Amy and me giggle. My sister and I have a close relationship, and coming up with a ridiculous nickname was appropriate considering the foundational trust we had created.

While we shouldn't hand out nicknames to *everyone* we see in a puddle, we can embrace humor when it feels right.

Amy and I would later laugh when our little brother, Andrew, modeled the many hats Amy had collected in preparation for her chemotherapy treatments. Andrew showed up that day with a freshly shaven head; he wanted to match his sister who would soon be losing her hair. What nineteen-year-old kid is that sweet? My little brother is. His bald, white head in a floppy sun hat was exactly the kind of ridiculous humor we needed that day.

Like Andrew, my fertility center also used humor to brighten a hard day. When I went to wash my hands after our first consultation, I saw that the sink was in the shape of a sperm; complete with a tail. Rob and I laughed hard over that one. Laughing feels good when life feels heavy.

WHEN WE ARE DISAPPOINTED

One of my best friends became pregnant before she was married. The biological father left the picture within months of hearing the news. My friend came from a conservative family where she had been taught that sex was reserved for marriage. She was scared to tell her parents that she was pregnant. Even though they were loving and kind, she knew the news would come as a shock and disappointment to them. I sat on pins and needles the first time she recapped the conversation for me.

"Mom, I'm pregnant," she said through her tears. On the other end of the phone, her mom expressed surprise and cried a little too. Then comes my favorite part. Knowing that the biological father was African American, her mom found the bright side of the situation. "Well honey," she said, "Growing up, you always talked about how cute black babies are. You said you wanted to adopt one someday. Now you don't have to!" They laughed and cried some more.

Because I also wanted to reserve physical intimacy for marriage, and I want the same for my kids, I can relate to both of these women's tears. Her mom could have been angry. She could have recited all the reasons she was disappointed in her daughter's choices. But she didn't.

What was done was done. There was no use in adding guilt to her child's already hurting heart. Mom was real, she cried, and she found a way to bring humor to the situation. I truly believe a good dose of humor makes a connection sweeter, and it can make someone feel seen.

CONNECTING THROUGH HUMOR

Embracing humor is a form of vulnerability. Letting ourselves relax enough to laugh and joke with people helps break down barriers and put us all on the same playing field. I agree with John Cleese when he said, "Laughter connects you with people. It's almost impossible to maintain any kind of distance or any sense of social hierarchy when you're just howling with laughter. Laughter is a force for democracy."

I am no expert on appropriate humor in stressful situations; hence the shortness of this chapter. I have made insensitive jokes in situations where I failed to keep my "too soon" wit to myself; however, I have seen humor bring hope.

Giggling about Delilah brought me hope. Hearing myself laugh brought me hope. We can bring that hope to others when they need us most.

Humor can bring people up for air when they're drowning. Like the plaque on Amy's wall reads, "Life is too important to be taken too seriously."

The Bottom Line

Humor is a great way to break up some of the heavy we all experience. Finding the funny in life and sharing it with those around us, might provide the moment of hope they need.

Chapter 12

Slowing Down

Mom, let's pretend I'm the Grinch and you're the monster!

—Sam, age 4

I dread playing imagination games with my kids.

Doing puzzles, playing board games, and reading books—I'm your girl. But the games my kids come up with—where I'm forced to play some made-up character they've come up with and say exactly what they tell me to, *word for word*—that turns my brain to mush. I feel like I'm back in science class, praying the school bell will ring so I can leave the torture chamber.

One reason I struggle to play imagination games is I feel like nothing is getting done. With a puzzle, board game, or book, I can see what we are accomplishing. I can measure the progress as we assemble puzzle pieces, move across a game board, and turn the pages of a book.

Playing robot dragons who can't decide if they want to be good guys or bad guys? It feels like nothing is getting done. It's just playing.

During a recent conversation with me, Rob pulled a cup from the cupboard, turned to get the milk out of our fridge, and turned back to fill the cup. The cup was gone.

I had already rinsed the cup and loaded it in the dishwasher, all while gabbing about something. I really like being productive. An empty glass screams at me to put it away. I also drive Rob crazy sometimes.

There are few things I love more than crossing off something on a to-do-list. I live for getting stuff done.

Learning the art of slowing down has helped me see others. Kids are great at teaching us how to slow down. They love to take their time with even the simplest of tasks. For a productivity junkie like myself, it's hard to stay patient when it takes them five minutes to do a task—like buckle their car seat—which I could have done in five seconds.

Most of my life, I saw staying ultra-busy as a strength. I packed my calendar so tight to ensure I was always doing something that felt productive. I thought it was smart to overbook myself so I felt challenged and never stayed idle.

The problem with keeping a relentless pace is it leaves little room for other people and their needs.

LEARNING TO PRESS PAUSE

My hips began hurting after I gave birth to my second child. When I could no longer ignore the pain, I sought out professionals—massage therapists, chiropractors, physical therapists, and an orthopedist. I learned I have something called hypermobility; or, as my orthopedist affectionately said, "You're like Gumby."

The joints in my shoulders, hips, and knees don't stabilize properly under high-impact exercise, like jumping and running. My muscles try to compensate for my wiggly joints, creating stress and pain in those areas. I was going to have to adjust the way I exercise. I had to slow down.

I was afraid and frustrated. I love the release of endorphins I get after a high-impact workout. Getting my heart rate up helps keep my mental health in a good spot. I was worried; if I slowed down, would my body produce the same euphoric chemicals?

I am happy to report that it did.

As I modified my exercises, I was able to intentionally focus on my form and body resistance. I flexed my muscles tighter. I kept good posture. I used my breath to push through challenging movements. Low impact workouts made me feel stronger than ever, and my heart rate was still high enough to release the endorphins.

I am falling in love with slowing down and working out with intention.

A LOW-IMPACT WAY OF LIFE

We live in a time of endless information and opportunities begging for our attention. We can easily cram our lives with work and entertainment, but we can find a better way to live. If we want to see others, we have to be willing to slow down our pace of life. We have to carve out time to *just be.* Just be together.

New York Times best-selling author Jerry Spinelli writes, "You haven't lived until you have basked in the adoration of people."[30] Basking doesn't strike me as a rushed action. Basking is relaxing, enjoying, and savoring. To see people, we have to take the time to be with them.

With my father's mental illness making it hard for him to work at times, our family struggled financially. One day, when I was still small, the doorbell rang. My mother opened the door to find a pair of brand-new dress shoes, exactly my size. While she never knew who left the shoes on our porch that day, Mom suspected it was someone from our church congregation. She wondered if they had helped me put my shoes on in the children's class; perhaps they noticed that my shoes were too tight. Mom felt seen that day, and I loved my special new shoes.

A stranger that I wish I could thank, slowed down enough to notice a little girl who needed bigger shoes. They slowed down enough to see parents who were struggling to put food on the table. The stranger wasn't too distracted by a never-ending to-do-list or a ringing phone; they lived slowly enough to see what was right in front of them. A family in need.

I will never forget the story of my new shoes. I am inspired by this stranger's ability to slow down enough to see a child, and a family, who needed some hope.

WHAT REALLY MATTERS

When Amy told us that her cancer had relapsed, I had to remind myself to breathe. After nine months of remission, the cancer was back, this time in her liver. She was given one or two years to live.

After I hung up the phone with her, I asked Rob to give me a few minutes alone. He took care of the kids while I let myself feel.

I was going to lose my sister, my confidant, and one of my greatest role models. She taught me how to be a mom. She taught me how to treat people with compassion. She taught me what it meant to be a committed spouse. We had been through so much together; I couldn't picture a life without her. I collapsed on the carpet. I began hitting and punching my bedroom floor. I listened to sad music. I cried and I cried and I cried.

I knew one thing immediately; I had *time*. I had time for her. Time to go on walks with her. Time to soak in her humor and grace. From that day forward, my activities became more deliberate and meaningful. While I was heartbroken at the thought of losing Amy, my life felt richer because I slowed down to see what, and more important, *who*, was most important.

Giving ourselves time to love others is perhaps one of the greatest gifts we can give. Just like low-impact exercise can help us move with greater precision, slowing down can allow us to feel and love *more* intensely, not less.

The Bottom Line

Slowing down gives us space to see other people and create meaningful connections with them.

Chapter 13

Loving with Intensity

*I do not know how to love in moderation.
My heart breathes a gentle intensity.*[31]

—Danielle Doby

I was walking out of the dollar store when it happened. Sam was two years old, toddling next to the stroller that carried his new baby sister. I'm not sure exactly how it happened, but in a distracted moment when I was looking the opposite direction, my hands slipped off the stroller and it rolled off the curb. I heard Sam's screams before I realized what I had done. I turned to see Sam's terrified face and his chubby little hands clutching the handlebars, trying desperately to keep the stroller from crashing into the cars driving by.

In a mama bear moment of epic proportions, I had the stroller and Sam in my arms in seconds. We were all safe and I was kicking myself for being so absentminded.

This story makes me teary as I type it. Not because of what could have happened if I hadn't grabbed the stroller and Sam in time, although it was a truly terrifying experience. I cry because of my Sam. I cry because of his intensity. He loved his baby sister, and he knew something bad could happen to her if we didn't stop the stroller.

The interesting thing about this story is that Sam was a very mixed up soul the day that Lydia was born. He was only mildly interested in her and absolutely furious with me. My sweet, mild-mannered angel had become something of a short-tempered troll. At seventeen-months-old, Sam took his first steps only days before I went into labor. While recovering from my second C-section, I couldn't pick him up for four weeks. I had to call neighbors to take him in and out of the crib or the bathtub. While I tried to normalize the situation by hugging him on the floor and eating meals together on the ground, he was not happy with the new arrangements. He was receiving less attention than he was used to and he hadn't seemed to make his mind up about this new baby. But none of that mattered when the stroller went rolling towards the street.

We can keep that same Sam-intensity when we engage in the work of truly *seeing* others. It doesn't matter what we think of each other, it matters that we remind each other of our purpose, that we engage in life together.

Sam wasn't strong enough to keep the stroller from rolling into the road. He couldn't do it by himself, but that didn't keep him from trying. His scream was an alarm to someone else—me. I was stronger and more capable of grabbing the stroller in time. But neither of us could have done that without the other. Sam was the siren, signaling that something was wrong and I was the one who could act.

When we see someone in distress, we can be sirens, calling for help from others who have the right skill sets to act. Both sirens and skills are needed in the work of saving people, whether it be physically or emotionally.

While isolation and disconnect can feel overwhelming in our culture's climate, we need to remember that we don't need to solve it alone. It's not all up to you, it's not all up to me. We can simply grab for the stroller and call out for help. Together, we can save each other from living lonely lives.

I want to tell you about some bad days I've had and how people's intensity kept me hanging on.

JUMPING IN

I will never forget a day when I was emotionally unraveling. My friend walked through my front door and saw me standing there in my living room. I must have looked as fatigued and defeated as I felt. I had nothing to give, no smile to reassure, and no fake words saying that "things will be okay." She didn't walk over to greet me; she *ran*. She grabbed me in her arms and she held me tight. You know that awkward part of a hug? The part when we try to gauge when the other person is easing up on their grip and starting to back away, to end the hug? None of that was happening on her end. She held me and held me and held me. She hugged me like she wanted to tell me something but words fell short. I could feel her soul speak to mine; this girl would do or give *anything* to ease a small part of my burden. She taught me what it means to get intense and jump in when people need us.

Because I was the recipient of that hug, I can tell you what it did for me. It served as a beacon of hope in the middle of darkness. Her intense love for me, in one of my worst moments, reminded me that I was worth fighting for. She was fighting for me, and it made me want to fight too.

We are all going to meet people who need a hug like that.

Don't let go too quick.

Let it be awkward.

Who even cares? At the end of the day, there will be no regrets for loving so hard.

LOVE SANDWICH

On a *different* rough day (I guess I've had a few), I was feeling isolated at home with only my toddlers to interact with. I needed some company. The last thing I wanted to do was invite myself to someone's house, but I looked at my precious littles and remembered that saving face didn't matter. I needed social interaction to stay healthy. I used that gift of mine and I opened my mouth.

I invited myself to my sister-in-law's house to spend the day. When the kids and I arrived, two sisters-in-law met me in the living room and asked how I was doing. As I began to speak, the sobbing came and the dam broke. My emotions took over and my body responded. My physical limbs began to collapse and I crumbled toward the ground. In an instant, one sister-in-law was holding me up from the back, and one from the front. It was a *love sandwich*. They cried, supporting my body as it shook from weeping. These two women physically held me up when I was all out of strength.

That is seeing someone.

What my sisters-in-law did that day didn't cure my psychological fatigue. It provided a moment of lightness; literally and figuratively. My heavy body was supported in their embrace. My mental vision of darkness was permeated with a glimpse of light. The light inside me felt almost nonexistent. But two women had light to share and I felt it around me as they held me up and cried with me. This moment was symbolic for me as I felt these women shoulder my burden.

My sisters-in-law and I, we are three very different people. We grew up in three different families, we are interested in different things, and we laugh at different jokes. We have gotten frustrated with each other. We have tried again. We have forgiven.

Let me tell you something, in a love sandwich, none of those differences mattered.

We can't let past disagreements, or differences of any kind keep us from participating in holding each other up, whether it's literal or figurative. We can love with intensity. We can snuggle in and engage in the power that comes from a love sandwich.

We might see our position shift in a love sandwich. If we are the one in the center, over time we will likely find ourselves on the outside, supporting someone else. If we are on the outside, there might come a time when we will need to fill the space in the middle.

We all need to get love-sandwiched once in a while.

STAGGERING BREAKS

While we can love with intensity, there will be times when our heart feels tired.

An important mentor shared an analogy with me that I have never forgotten. As a specialist in the army, he observed intense teamwork exercises on the base. Let me explain how this particular drill works.

Picture a massive log, something like a telephone pole. Now picture a squad holding the log over their heads. Now picture them jogging in line formation across a long distance. It's an exercise that requires extreme mental and physical endurance. It would be impossible for any individual to complete it alone, or even together without breaks. The only way to complete the goal is for each soldier to have resting periods during the run. As the group carries the log above their heads, one recruit pulls out of the line and jogs in the back, giving his arms a break from lifting the log. The short rest refreshes him just enough to be able to jump back in and carry the log with his comrades. Then another recruit does the same. They rotate through the soldiers in order to stagger their individual breaks without interrupting the forward progression towards the destination. To be successful, each person must carry to their limit of strength and then rest when they can't give anymore. If each individual does this with precision, the group will never have to set the log down or stop jogging. They will reach their destination, fatigued but victorious.

Each of us will have the opportunity to carry the burdens life will inevitably bring. Sometimes it will be our own burden we are carrying; sometimes it will be someone else's that we are lifting. No doubt, it is an intense work we are a part of and to be successful, everyone needs reprieve sometimes. Nobody can carry and run forever without burning out.

ROOM FOR DESSERT

In the film *Finding Forrester*, Sean Connery portrays an accomplished novelist. Upon seeing him reading *The National Inquirer*, his pupil asks him, "How come a guy like you wastes his time reading *The National Inquirer*? It's trash . . . you should be reading . . . *The Times*." Sean Connery responds, "I read *The Times* for dinner. But this, this is my dessert."[32]

To love with intensity, we have to make room for dessert. My dessert is an evening on the couch-watching a movie with popcorn and a Diet Coke. What's yours?

My friend works with terminally ill cancer patients as her full-time job, and she loves it. But when she goes home, she doesn't watch movies about cancer. Why? Because her job *is* cancer. She knows that she has to take a break from cancer or she won't be able to perform and love with the amount of intensity her patients need. When she goes home, she takes a break from the heaviness of her job. She watches comedies, not dramas. Her full-time job helping cancer patients is her dinner. Watching funny movies is her dessert. Laughing at a comedy helps her rest up; she comes back to work the next day refreshed and eager to be fully present with her patients. When we make room for dessert, we re-energize so we can love with intensity another day.

It is with this same intensity *and* awareness of our limits that we need to love the people around us. We don't have to deprive ourselves of breaks or dessert; in fact, we won't be successful if we do. We will be victorious when we balance loving with intensity and resting when we need to regroup. Taking breaks is a way to create healthy boundaries for ourselves, so we can see people better. We can carry the log, take a break, and hop back in.

The Bottom Line

The connections we create in moments of crisis will change our relationships with people forever. When we jump in to help someone hurting *and* stagger our breaks, we can love with a greater intensity.

Chapter 14

Boundaries

*If empathy without boundaries is self-destruction,
then empathy with boundaries is compassion.*[33]

—WellnessLabAndClinics.com

As an educator and parent, one of the most important things I've learned is that kids need structure. Their developing brains want to know what to expect, what to plan for; they *like* boundaries. You and I are just big kids. We are in the driver's seat and we get to create perfect, individualized boundaries based on our needs. Life isn't quite as simple as it was in second grade, but we have grown more complex along with it.

WHAT IS A BOUNDARY?

A boundary is a way of marking our limits. Boundaries can be spoken. For example, I set a boundary with my kids when I say, "If you hit me, you will go to time out." Boundaries can also be unspoken, a commitment we make to ourselves like, "I am going to bed at 10:00 p.m., whether or not the football game is over."

HOW DO WE SET UP A BOUNDARY?

While there are many step-by-step guides on how to set up a boundary, I like this simple three-step plan:

Establish what we want.

Communicate what we want.

Honor what we want.

For example: Perhaps I spend a lot of the day answering emails for work, long after my eight-hour shift. I know that people value my timely responses, but my home life is suffering because when I'm there, I'm often distracted by messages from work.

Establishing what I want—I want to be more present when I come home from work.

Communicating what I want—I tell my coworkers that I will be happy to answer their emails during my normal work hours, from 8:00 to 5:00 p.m. At 5:00 p.m., I won't be checking my email for the rest of the evening.

Honoring what I want—At 5:00 p.m., I turn off my work email and don't check it until 8:00 a.m. the next morning.

THE PURPOSE

Boundaries are similar to physical fences. Two main reasons to install a fence are to increase the value and safety of the property.

The purpose of boundaries is no different. Boundaries improve our relationships and keep us safe.

BOUNDARIES ARE COMPASSIONATE

Boundaries are a way of demonstrating compassion in a relationship. They keep connections healthy and trustworthy because everybody knows what to expect.

Brené Brown says, "Compassionate people ask for what they need. They say no when they need to, and when they say yes, they mean it. They're compassionate because their boundaries keep them out of resentment."[34]

Sometimes, a boundary is as simple as the word "no." I have a friend who is a great example of how to keep relationships strong by saying "no" when she needs to. Not too long ago, I texted her, *Hey, want to have a girl's night?* She responded honestly, *Tonight doesn't work. My husband and I need some alone time to hang out and be together.*

Why is saying "no" to a friend compassionate? It gives us confidence in our relationship because when the other person says yes, we know they mean it. Our relationships are more meaningful when we trust the other person is telling the truth.

When my friend compliments me, I believe her, and I feel two inches taller. Keeping healthy boundaries gets easier as we see our relationships blossom because of it.

We can invite people into our lives who aren't afraid of boundaries. We can trust them. If we ask them for a favor, they will say no if they can't do it. They won't do it because they feel obligated and then resent us. The best relationships we have include respect for each other's boundaries. Instead of second-guessing each other, we can spend our energy connecting.

BOUNDARIES KEEP US OUT OF *THE HOLE*

When my therapist told me that she tried not to think about me on the weekends, it hurt.

I didn't want to feel alone. It scared me to think that she went on living while I was stuck in the bottom of this *hole*. I wanted someone to be with me in my turmoil, to know what I felt. But she taught me that nobody can help you if they get down in the hole, because then they can't get out themselves.

"The hole" is the place you live when you don't have hope. I've been there; maybe you've been there yourself. My friend refers to it as "the upside down." If you are a *Stranger Things* fan, you know the hole is a tough place to live.

When someone is in the hole for whatever reason, it's hard for them to see a way out. It's hard to believe the sun still shines because they can't see the light from down there. They look around and all they see is darkness. They wonder if it will all crumble down on top of them and they won't make it out alive.

Wise allies know they cannot get in the hole with the person they are helping. If my therapist were to get in the hole with me, she explained, "I would be no use to you in there."

We run the risk of getting in the hole with someone when, in an effort to save them, we don't take care of ourselves. When I found out Amy was dying from cancer, I cried every day for weeks. That grieving was important. But after a few weeks, my grieving began to turn from meaningful to destructive.

I felt the pull of the hole. When I woke up, I didn't want to get out of bed and do my normal routine of morning exercise. I wanted to pull the covers over my head and stay there all day. I started questioning the purpose of life and lacked the motivation to hope.

What kept me from slipping in the hole? The forethought that my sister and her family were going to need my help. I wouldn't be any help to them if I was in the hole. I set up boundaries for myself that kept me mentally healthy, which included getting out of bed and daily exercise.

Different circumstances can push people in the hole. What affects you negatively might not affect me in the same way. A few years ago, my husband and I were watching a movie at the theatre. When it finished, my husband turned to ask me how I'd liked the film, to find me weeping and pushing off a panic attack. In shock, we both realized that what had been an interesting story to him, proved to be a triggering experience for me. We have to know ourselves to stay on solid ground.

The best place for us to help someone out of the hole is at the top of it.

At the top of the hole, we can listen, empathize, and most important, just sit there. We can assure the person, "There is sunshine up here; you will see it again!" We stay in a healthy mindset close to the sun where we avoid slipping in the hole ourselves.

Staying out of the hole is a boundary, and it's a critical one. If we want to help somebody in the hole, we can throw down a proverbial ladder. A ladder could be helping our friend in the hole make an important appointment or share an uplifting song. We can listen to them, take them out for ice cream, and cheer them on. Watching our friend climb out of the hole and into the sunshine again will be worth our efforts.

In the spirit of authenticity, I'll tell you that in my experience there is only one person who can get in the hole with someone else and not get hurt themselves.

And His name is Jesus.

MINDFUL LIMITS

Mindfulness, a practice extracted from Buddhism, is key when creating boundaries. Mindfulness is the practice of observing our thoughts without judgment. Mindfulness is living in the present. Mindfulness has well-researched benefits and is a powerful tool that helps us identify where we need boundaries.

A simple way to think about mindfulness is living in the present moment. What do the rings on the inside of the carrot look like after you take a bite? What does the hand soap in the employee break room smell like? What noises do you hear in the trees? We can watch our thoughts like clouds drifting by in the sky. Mindfulness can help us stay grounded in the now, which is the only place we can improve.

Grounding in the now helped my friend comfort his child during a dangerous situation and set up a necessary boundary.

One afternoon, my friend attempted to cross a busy street with his seven-year-old daughter. As he looked left and right at the intersection, his daughter stepped onto the road towards the oncoming traffic. Terrified, he pulled her from the street and set her on the sidewalk. He shook her by the shoulders and reprimanded her. She trembled and her eyes grew big. Her father's anger scared her. Because he had been learning to be mindful, he stopped himself, realizing that fearful thoughts were dictating his behavior. He pulled his daughter into a hug and said, "I'm sorry. I'm not mad at you; I was terrified that I almost lost you." He then set up a boundary. "Don't cross the street unless I tell you to." Observing his thoughts helped him recognize the fear beneath his anger and where he needed a boundary.

BOUNDARIES INSTEAD OF FIXING PEOPLE

Do we find ourselves in situations where we try to fix people? Do we convince ourselves that if we work harder, we can fix them? The problem with this thought is, first–it's not true. Nobody can force someone else to change. When we try to control someone else, we don't fix them. Instead, we can end up feeling fatigued and stressed. Second, other people's feelings are not our responsibility. Third, nobody likes how it feels when someone is trying to fix them. It's a bad recipe for nurturing connection.

When we feel bad for someone who is in a hard situation, we can redirect our focus. Instead of draining our energy supply by trying to fix them, we can look at ourselves and determine what we can offer. We show them compassion, we connect with them, and we keep boundaries where they are needed.

We all need to remind ourselves what a therapist once reminded me. "Julie, you cannot fix other people. That is not your job. There is only *one* person in this world that can do that and you aren't Him." She was right. I am not Jesus and neither are you.

The Bottom Line

Boundaries strengthen relationships and keep us safe as we help others. We can mindfully set limits which keep us from slipping in the hole and trying to fix people.

Chapter 15

We Can't Fix It

I can find only three kinds of business in the universe:
mine, yours, and God's. Much of our stress comes
from mentally living out of our business.[35]

—Byron Katie

IT'S NOT ABOUT THE NAIL

My husband and I love a YouTube video called "It's Not About the Nail."[36] We laugh so hard at the video clip because what it showcases is *so true* about our marriage. The video shows a woman complaining about the pressure she feels and how she fears it will never stop. The camera shifts revealing a nail protruding from her forehead. The man (presumably her husband) is sitting next to her on the couch, nodding. When he suggests that the nail is responsible for her pain and suggests they remove it, she responds, "You always do this, you always try to fix things!" and "It's not about the nail!"

Y'all need to go watch it.

While men are stereotyped for their "trying to fix it" badge of honor, I think we all have times when we want to fix each other. We go into fix-it-mode especially when someone we care about is hurting.

Even kids want to fix things. Let me share a pivotal experience that helped me give up my fix-it-badge for good.

FIXING MY CHILDHOOD

Some of my favorite memories of my childhood happened in Goblin Valley State Park, located in Emery County, Utah. The gigantic bowl of natural goblin-like rock formations proved to be the best place for a classic game of Sardines, with endless boulders to climb on, jump off, and hide behind. We loved going camping as a family. I still remember my older brother telling us scary stories around the campfire, convincing me that the rock formations did indeed transform into goblins at night. I still feel sentimental when I eat Strawberry Twizzlers and Sunbelt chocolate chip granola bars, the food staples I remember best from our family camping trips. It was magical, and I treasure memories like these.

And as mentioned previously, our family was not free from struggle and suffering.

When I was five years old, I bounced through the door as I returned from kindergarten, a brown paper lunch bag on my hand—a farm animal puppet of some sort that I have since forgotten. I walked into my parents' room and saw my dad lying completely still on his bed. His eyes were wide open, but he didn't blink. His gaze was fixed on the ceiling.

I remember climbing up on the bed to show him my puppet, but his paralyzed stare and expression didn't change. I didn't understand what was wrong. Why couldn't I wake him up? Why couldn't I fix this? My older sister, who was ten at the time, later confided that she thought he was dead when she saw him. She pounded on his chest, begging him to wake up. She wanted to fix it too. I count myself fortunate that I was more confused than scared in this moment. I don't think I was old enough to comprehend that my dad could be dead.

But he wasn't dead. After about a half hour, he regained consciousness. He had been in a depression-induced catatonic state. Catatonia is a behavioral syndrome marked by an inability to move normally. It can be associated with schizophrenia and other mental illnesses.

My father's depressive episodes were severe and relentless; he endured many difficult years. While seeing him in a catatonic state was an isolated, one-time experience, I remember it so clearly that it is usually the first thought that comes to mind when I think of my childhood. Why do I remember it so well? Because it was shocking, and my brain couldn't process *why* I couldn't fix it.

Not being able to fix someone we love can feel out of control and scary. But the good news is that we *can* control something. We *can* control our willingness to come to the table with love and compassion for everyone involved. We *can* lean into the vulnerability that lack of control brings and make sure no one goes unseen.

This memory is one small part of my childhood and there is nothing to fix. It just *is*. I feel compassion for my dad and every member of my family in that memory, including the kindergartener. It still makes me sad when I think about her on that day. There is nothing wrong with feeling sad sometimes. We don't need to fix negative feelings, we need to process them. We need to allow other people the same room to process their emotions.

ALLOWING EMOTIONS

I have tried to deal with unwanted emotions in two different ways— leaning *away* from them and leaning *into* them. Leaning away from my emotions didn't make them disappear, the emotions just came out later in more complicated ways. I don't recommend leaning away from emotions.

I've learned that the fastest and healthiest way to deal with unwanted emotions is to lean into them.

It is important that we allow others to lean into their emotions too.

When my child walks in the door crying because he scraped his knee, I don't tell him that it doesn't hurt. I do my best to empathize and understand. "I'm sorry it hurts. Can I get you some ice?" The quicker I validate his pain, the quicker he wipes his eyes and runs out to play.

We can allow others to feel their emotions so they can get through them successfully and move forward.

EMPATHY AND CONFIDENCE

If we try to fix someone's problem, we run the risk of missing the opportunity to see them, and hurting them in the process. We humans want to feel understood and validated in our feelings. When we don't feel validated in our feelings, we are more likely to dig in our heels and justify how bad we feel. It's important to take time to make sure the person in conflict feels seen. Saying things like, "I see you" and "That makes sense" communicate the compassion and connection they seek. When someone feels validated, they are more likely to pull themselves out of the situation and find positive solutions.

When we try to fix someone, we might be implying that we don't have confidence that the person can solve their own problems. We show faith in them by sitting with them and showing compassion. We can have full confidence that they can pull through. The people we help have found ways to cope in the past. They have a 100% track record of getting through hard things, or else they wouldn't be standing in front of us. We can trust that they can get through this too.

GIVING ENCOURAGEMENT

An unlikely person taught me how to encourage, without trying to fix it.

During my bouts of anxiety and depression, there were times when Rob and I struggled to understand each other. He tried to *fix it* and I, in turn, felt ashamed that I needed fixing. I resolved to work even harder to fix it myself without depending on him. We knew we loved each other, and we stumbled along as we tried to figure out how to work through this together.

In desperation, I went to the doctor, who prescribed a new antidepressant for me. That night as my husband and I sat on our couch feeling confused and scared, a knock came at the door. We opened it and were surprised to find a guy from our neighborhood. He stood at 6'2" with a shaved head, broad shoulders, and a beard; an image that screamed "run away from me." Previously, I had thought of him as reserved, gruff, and intimidating.

At our house, we referred to him as "The Scary Guy."

He said he felt like he should stop by our house, then asked me directly, "Julie, how are you?" When "the scary guy" asks you a question, you answer. I began to cry. He looked into my eyes and said, "You're really struggling, huh? Things are pretty bad?" He understood. I felt his compassion and complete attention. He was seeing me, really seeing me. The tightness in my chest began to release. He told me about *his* experience with depression and anxiety. He knew what I was going through. He recognized the hell where I was living; he had once lived there too. He shouldered my cross with me and illuminated the hope ahead.

"You can do it," he told me, "I know you feel like there is no way out, but I promise there is." I sobbed even harder. From my hole, I saw a glimmer of light shining above me. Maybe the sun was still shining, even though I couldn't see it. But he could see it and I believed him. I asked him over and over again, "Are you *really* happy now? I'll be happy again? You promise me?"

He promised.

I wasn't the only one who needed encouragement. Rob asked him, "What can I do for her? I don't know what to say to her." The Scary Guy told him, "Love her. Listen to her. It's going to be rough while she is waiting for this new medicine to kick in. Be nice to her." He was telling Rob to open his eyes and *see me. Don't fix her, see her.*

This experience was pivotal in my healing process and in my marriage. The Scary Guy was willing to be vulnerable and dive into our uncomfortable space in order to really see us in our challenges.

After such an intimate experience, I decided it was time I call him by his real name, Chris.

SIT WITH THEM

Jennie Taylor taught me an important lesson about not "fixing it." Jennie is the wife of Major Brent Taylor, previous mayor of North Ogden City, Utah. Amid his deployment in 2018, Major Taylor was killed during an insider attack in Afghanistan, leaving his wife a widow and his seven children fatherless.

While Jennie and I were speaking at an event in San Diego, she told me she had to learn that nothing will fix her husband's death. Not a new marriage, no amount of life insurance money, no number of casseroles, nothing. Nothing will ever fix the fact that her husband is gone. However, she still holds onto hope. She feels hope when she can sit with someone and tell them how much she misses her husband, without them telling her how she can fix it. She feels hope when people don't treat her like she is something to be fixed. She has learned that there is nothing wrong with feeling sad. She can *feel* her feelings without someone trying to push them aside. Instead of *fixing it,* she needs space to *face it.*

The organization that flew me out to speak at this event knew about Amy's terminal cancer diagnosis, and they offered to fly her out too. We had a great sister weekend together. The highlight of my weekend was watching Amy and Jennie Taylor meet. Jennie wrote this about the experience:

> Meeting Amy was one of the most humbling experiences of my widowhood. . . . Amy has six kids. And she is dying. She knows she is dying. She doesn't know how much time she still has, but she knows her time here is running out.
>
> When I met and embraced Amy, it's as if the world once again flipped inside, outside, and upside down. We laughed and we cried. Sometimes simultaneously. We spoke directly to each other's souls with genuine and very personal compassion. Sometimes we used words, but mostly our hearts didn't need words to make that connection. Amy and I are certain our paths didn't cross by mere coincidence. We both felt strengthened by meeting each other and seeing in each other the reassuring truth that we can do hard things. We both left comforted in knowing that we are not the only ones facing tragedy and trials in life. It's not a matter of misery loving company; rather, there's a strength to be found in knowing that others are also fighting the good fight, and even finding joy in the journey.[37]

Jennie and Amy were in their own world, a world where it was okay not to fix it. Their example of seeing each other with love and acceptance is a moment I'll never forget.

We can breathe a sigh of relief. We don't need to *fix* people's problems. We can love them *through* their problems instead.

The Bottom Line

We ditch *trying to fix it* when we allow ourselves and others to feel all the feelings without guilt or expectation. We weren't born to fix others, we were born to see people, to connect with them and to have compassion on them.

Part Five

Looking Closer

Chapter 16

Enhancing Our View

There are always flowers for those who want to see them.[38]

—Henri Matisse

The first television was invented in 1927. The inventor, Philo Taylor Farnsworth, was only twenty-one years old. Nobody cared that the picture was in black and white. Black and white was all they knew, and it was exciting.[39]

SEEING IN BLACK AND WHITE

I've been known to cut people off when I am driving.

I don't cut people off because I'm trying to be rude. No, I'm not a good enough driver to be purposely unkind. I cut people off because my brain is thinking seventy-three thoughts at once and sometimes I am completely oblivious to the other driver's presence.

What store had produce on sale today? How many minutes until I need to pick up Sam from preschool? What am I making for dinner? Did I close the garage door? What if I forget to write something important in my book? When was the last time Rob and I went on a date? What is Lydia sticking up her nose back there?

During one particular incident, the other driver screamed profanities at me (which I didn't understand) and gifted me the middle
finger. While I am always striving to be a more courteous driver, I
mostly tried to remember the profanities so I could ask Rob what they
all meant when I saw him.

I came home and received the protective validation from my husband that I wanted; we concluded that the other driver was a jerk.
(Drivers like me make Rob crazy, but when it's me getting yelled at,
he's more angry that someone swore at his wife).

I felt wronged. I told myself the other driver was mean and I was
nice. I was thinking in black and white. Black and white thinking is
thinking about people in absolutes; good or bad, mean or nice, wrong
or right. Black and white thinking denies the ability to hold more
than one emotion at once. When I think in black and white, there is
no in-between.

FALSE SAFETY

By thinking of myself as "good" and the other driver as "bad," I feel
safe. I elevate myself above the rude, embarrassing behavior I just witnessed. I like the safe feeling I get when I think about people in black
and white.

The problem with feeling safe in black and white thinking is this:
all of us will experience situations that don't make sense in black and
white. Life is too complicated for just two colors.

I grew up watching families whose parents got divorced. It's hard
to admit, but deep down, I assumed those families were doomed for
unhappiness.

My parents went through a divorce three years ago, and I became
part of a severed family. Do I engage in the black and white thinking
that my brain feeds me? *Families where parents stay together are always
happy? Families with divorced parents are bound to be miserable?*

All of a sudden, things feel confusing; my situation doesn't fit
neatly in my black and white mindset. Life hardly ever turns out how
we think it will. While I do believe in *some* absolute truths, my life

experience continues to teach me that this existence is messy and complicated. And that's not so bad. What it *is*, is real.

What's interesting about thinking in black and white to feel safe, is that it's actually not safe at all. When we thrive in black and white thinking, we can fall flat on our face when we discover that way of thinking doesn't hold up. Maybe we learn that our boss at work has been embezzling money from the company, all while being an incredible leader that taught integrity to his employees. Maybe our spouse breaks a promise. Maybe we make a mistake that goes against what we teach our children.

Black and white thinking won't save us in these situations. Black and white thinking makes hard things *harder*. When there is no room in our brain for multiple feelings and multiple realities happening all at once, shocking experiences can demolish our belief system and leave us saying the all too famous sentiment: *I don't know what I believe anymore.*

When we allow ourselves to feel multiple emotions at once, we are able to come to the table with an open mind instead of thinking in absolutes. An open mind leaves room and time to find what is true.

MULTIPLE EMOTIONS AT ONCE

I got a lot of ear infections as a kid. I would wake up in the middle of the night with my ears throbbing. They hurt so much; the only thing that helped the pain was a blow dryer. I spent many nights lying in my mother's arms as she held a hot blow dryer close to my ear. The heat soothed the pain, and I loved the one-on-one attention from my mom. She sang "The Ants Go Marching" and patted my back with a steady beat.

I soothe my own children with the same patting rhythm.

Both I, as the child, and my mother, experienced more than one emotion at once during my nights of ear infections. We both hated that I was miserable, *and* we both loved the time to bond.

I feel the same way with my own children. I passed on my bad ears; they have suffered with ear infections since birth. Before getting tubes put in their ears (hallelujah), I spent many hours holding them through the throbbing pain. They didn't want to do anything but be held. We watched movies together, took naps together, and read books together. I hated seeing my babies suffer *and* I loved the snuggles that came with it.

We can feel more than one thing at once, which means we can recognize that people make both good and bad decisions.

SEEING IN COLOR

In 1954, America watched as the Michigan State Spartans beat the UCLA Bruins 28–20 in full color. The annual Rose Bowl football game was the first "colorcast," and television watching would never be the same.[40]

Seeing in color is recognizing the complexities of another's circumstances and feeling compassion for them.

I think we can all agree that when I cut the driver off, his response was less than compassionate. But when I am thinking in black and white, I'm not being compassionate either. My brain says, *What a punk! That driver is a bad person, I would never do that.* But here's where it gets complicated. What if that person is coming from the hospital after losing a loved one? What if he just lost his job? What if he just exchanged harsh words with a parent? What if he doesn't think anybody sees him?

Would that knowledge change the fact that his actions were unkind? No. But when I picture the possible reasons for his outburst, things don't feel so clear to me. It's unsettling. Because all of a sudden I am feeling one of the Big C's. Compassion.

Oh, crap.

That's another C word I say a lot.

Seeing people in color takes intention at first, but it doesn't take long before your eyes prefer it. Colored vision helps us *see* the people who need us. I can feel compassion for the angry driver *and* feel hurt by his comments. I don't have to choose. He's not bad and he's not good. He just *is*.

What will come when we choose to see people in color instead of black and white? We will *see* people everywhere. It will feel like freedom because now we don't have to play tug-of-war with our emotions; we can let them all show up at once. We might even have room to notice the good others have to offer.

SEEING IN HIGH DEFINITION

In 1998, we were all blown away when high definition television (HDTV) became available. The world watched the first HDTV broadcast that year—the launch of the space shuttle Discovery and John Glenn's return to space. To date, John was the oldest person to go into space at age 77. The world watched the space mission in high definition.[41]

Seeing in high definition is recognizing the strengths people offer.

Black and White Thinking → Color → High Definition

In the last few years, Rob has started wearing glasses with a slight prescription. He often looks at me and says, "Whoa, it's Julie in high-def!" I like to think he is seeing me, not only in color, but with greater vibrancy. My eyes are bluer, and let us hope that my teeth are whiter.

Seeing people in high definition means we are able to not only recognize the complicated circumstances of their lives (color), but we can recognize the gifts they have which benefit the world (high definition). We become teachable to the lessons they have to offer.

Remember how a lot of us felt when we finished the film *Avatar*? Looking around, our world looked dull in comparison to the mind-blowing, colorful world we had just witnessed. The Na'vi people were *so* blue, and their flowers *so* red. That's the kind of high definition I want for my life, and yours too.

FINDING TRUTH IN OTHERS

I was listening to Oprah interview a famous actor while doing my dishes. Before the interview began, I had stereotyped the celebrity in my head as a person who lacked authenticity and deep thinking. I assumed he was fake because of his money and fame.

I had watched him on the big screen and knew some of the roles he had played. I had watched him say and do things I wouldn't do. The personal choices he made didn't agree with mine. From the outside, his "moral code" looked different than mine and part of me thought, *there isn't anything I can gain from listening to his interview.* I told myself that I should be listening to someone who was more in line with my moral belief system.

But, I listened.

The longer I listened to the interview, the more I found myself liking the actor. I found the interview both powerful and uplifting. I felt more committed to my own beliefs. The interview helped me pause to ponder my love for God and all human beings. It was a heart-warming thirty minutes of my time well spent.

This experience didn't fit in a neat package with a bow. I questioned myself: why was I experiencing so much inner turmoil about listening to an interview that was creating positive feelings? Over time, the answer dawned on me. I was thinking in black and white: *either I listen to people who match my belief system identically, or I am listening to something I shouldn't.*

It's almost as if I was listening to the actor and thinking: *What a waste. He has such good advice; it's too bad he is automatically wrong because I don't agree with all of his decisions.* That, my friends, is black and white thinking.

Someone can be wrong about one thing and right about another. While it seems obvious, we can subconsciously forget this principle. We each have light to share and we *also* make mistakes. I can be speaking to an audience and say something that is pure truth and people feel that truth so hard; they feel it resonate in their bones. And one hour later, I can be at home, belittling my husband. The fact that I belittle my husband one hour later does not take away the fact that what I said to that audience is *still true.* But my critical thoughts like to tell me that I have no place sharing light that night, when I was so quick to make a mistake.

False.

We live in a world of complex, beautiful, surprising people.

I'm glad on that day, that I was able to stop myself from thinking in black and white and take in the truth the actor was teaching. I reaped the benefits of his life lessons learned and was able to see him as someone like me—a fellow traveler on this journey of life, doing the best he can. I was taught a powerful truth that day. Just because someone acts or thinks differently than us, does not mean that they don't have truth to share. *(Que Pocahontas Soundtrack, "You think the only people who are people, are the people who look and think like you.")*

A mantra in the meditation world is "just be." Truth is the expert of what it means to "just be." Truth is truth. Truth is unemotional. Truth is not loaded with judgements or fears. Truth just *is* and truth always will *be*. If we look for it, we will see that people of all varieties have pieces of truth to offer us.

One consistent thing I notice in all the people I have met and interviewed is that they each have a history unlike any other story I have ever heard. Each person is fascinating, a compilation of unique life experiences. In my mind, a room full of distinct, complicated people with stories to share . . . well, I can't think of a more beautiful sight. Can you?

THE FEAR OF LOVE

We are bound to love people more when we see them in high definition. We become more heavily invested in relationships, which creates more risk and vulnerability. We could get hurt. That's how love works. All the same, it's worth making the investment and taking the risk.

In her book, *The Fear of Flying*, Erica Jong wrote, "Do you want me to tell you something really subversive? Love is everything it's cracked up to be. That's why people are so cynical about it. It really is worth fighting for, being brave for, risking everything for. And the trouble is, if you don't risk anything, you risk even more."[42]

Seeing people in high definition will fill our lives with love and light. After all, we know we need light to see color. It will open our eyes to the unending possibilities for friendships. The compassion that we feel for people who struggle is a gift worth fighting for. Seeing people as humans who are doing their best with the hand they've been dealt, will serve us well.

The most exciting part of ditching black and white thinking is we no longer have to wait for others to be like us to see them. We can connect and be compassionate, all while standing firmly in what we believe.

COMPASSION AND CONSEQUENCES

I have a dear family friend who served as a district judge for close to a decade. In a recent conversation, he reminded me, "Compassion and love can mean, in the appropriate circumstances, letting the person hit rock bottom."

There *is* good and bad behavior. When a stranger kidnaps a child at a playground, they are making a bad choice. Their complicated upbringing doesn't diminish their bad behavior. This is an important distinction to make. Seeing in color and high definition doesn't mean we excuse bad behavior; it means we have compassion for the person who made the choice and allow important consequences to follow.

No matter the person or the choice, there is always more to learn about people.

The Bottom Line

Black and white thinking creates disconnection. We see people in color by recognizing the complexities of their lives and having compassion on them. This allows us to relate with them and find common ground, which in turn forges connection. We see people in high definition when we recognize their strengths and how they benefit the world.

Chapter 17

The Hand We Are Dealt

Do the best you can until you know better.
Then when you know better, do better.[43]

—Maya Angelou

When I heard a rumor that Santa Claus wasn't real, I evaded the subject all together. I was scared I had been wrong, that I'd believed in someone who only existed in my imagination. I chose not to look at the possibility for years. But in the back of my mind, there lived a growing anxiety that there wasn't a chubby man in a red suit who flew around the world in a sleigh.

However, when I learned the truth about Santa, I also learned the truth about who *had* filled my stockings. I saw my parents in a new way; they were playing Santa Claus because they wanted to bring me joy. The news wasn't *all* bad.

It took courage to sit my parents down and ask, "Is Santa real?" But I decided that I'd rather know the truth—even if it made me sad—rather than believe a myth. Brené Brown says, "You can choose courage or you can choose comfort; you cannot have both."[44] While expanding our perspective can sometimes be unsettling, the light it brings changes how we *see* the people around us.

As humans, we constantly have to make judgements to inform our decisions. It's important to recognize there is always more than meets the eye. There is more story, more meaning, and more humanity.

OUR CARDS

We each come to life's game table with a different deck of cards. Our cards are the components that affect how we see the world around us. These components can be where we grew up, our family of origin, our birth order, hereditary traits, our exposure to different people and situations, our heartaches, our victories, our mental health, our physical health—all of it and more combine to create personal convictions. As we interact with others, it is impossible to know all the reasons they think and believe what they do. We will never be able to *truly* "walk a mile in their shoes;" a mile wouldn't be long enough to get the whole picture.

Most of us want to stand up for what we believe is right. What we term as "right" has a lot to do with the elements listed above. As we strive to *see* others, it's vital that we remember that nobody's mind works exactly like ours, because nobody's story is just like ours. We each deserve compassion as we try and figure out this life together.

If we are hesitant to listen to someone based on the causes they do or don't support, we can remember that our differences make us powerful. There are experiences from our lives that make us passionate about our convictions. I am passionate about *seeing* people because people saved my life by doing just that. Tim Ballard is passionate about saving children from trafficking, because he was exposed to the horror of it. My brother and sister-in-law are passionate about giving blood because their daughter's life was dependent on blood transfusions.

It's a *good* thing we each come to the table with a different deck of cards. Our unique convictions motivate us to make the world a better place. We need as many perspectives as possible to unify humanity.

FINDING MORE

I dragged myself to a workout class before the sun was out. I was surprised by the chipperness of the fitness instructor, who seemed unaware that it was 5:30 *in the morning*. Throughout the class I questioned whether her positive encouragement was genuine, or if she was playing the part she thought her class expected. After an hour of sweat and burpees, I concluded she was just playing a part; no one could truly feel that enthusiastic at such an hour.

I ran into the instructor a few weeks later. She recognized me from her class. As we introduced ourselves, I learned new information. She had been divorced twice. She was a single mom of four kids. And through her own challenges, she had learned the importance of self-compassion and self-development. She explained that her experiences were the reason she encouraged her classes the way she did; she had fought hard to love herself and she extended that love to others.

I walked away from our conversation feeling both inspired and sheepish. I had made an assumption about her based on one experience. I didn't know enough to make such a verdict. When I learned more about my instructor, I recognized that I was wrong. She wasn't playing a part; she was teaching the self-compassion she fought for in her own life.

Our perspective changes when we listen.

Is it easier to slap labels on peoples' heads (if you're a fan of *The Office*, you know the episode I'm thinking of), rather than get to know them? Yes. It is easier. But we aren't looking for easy, we are looking for the truth about people. People who are different from us can widen our perspective and help us discover more truth. They can help us become the best, most well-informed versions of ourselves.

One of my favorite quotes comes from the Dr. Seuss book, *The Sneetches*. It's a story about a group of creatures who separate themselves by having or not having stars on their bellies.

> The Sneetches got really quite smart on that day. The day they decided that Sneetches are Sneetches. And no kind of Sneetch is the best on the beaches. That day, all the Sneetches forgot about stars and whether they had one, or not, upon thars.[45]

When it comes to seeing people, no matter their opinions and actions, our first priority needs to be unconditional love. Other priorities can follow, but we should never allow them to overshadow our first. Most people are doing the best they can with the hand they've been dealt. We can give each other a pass as we navigate our complicated human history. We can lean into curiosity *together*, because one thing we know—there is always more to learn.

The Bottom Line

We can look at people with wonder instead of criticism and watch our vision dramatically improve. Our perspective broadens when we are willing to learn. Truth will make itself known the *more* we know, not less.

Chapter 18

Conviction to Listen

We're paying the highest tribute we can pay a man.
We trust him to do right. It's that simple.[46]

—Harper Lee, *To Kill a Mockingbird*

A group of people united in a common cause is breathtaking. No matter our religion, political party or horoscope, we can unite in one common cause to listen to each other.

While our society wrestles with complex issues that have the power to drive us apart, when we are willing to listen to each other—especially when we disagree—hearts and generations can mend. We each have our own declarations to share. We *all* deserve the right to share our convictions and be heard.

RACIAL EQUALITY

There are diverse races across the planet, each deserving our love and respect. Two races that have a complex history are African Americans and Caucasions; or more commonly referred to as black and white.

At times, I have heard both black and white people share frustration. Some of my white friends tell me they're sick of the "race conversation" because they leave these exchanges feeling like they will always be the bad guys, no matter how long it's been since the Civil War. They say they don't look at black people as "less than;" they want to be on even ground and move forward. They don't want to be judged by their white skin color, or because of the choices of people they never knew nor agreed with. I see you, my white friends. I get that.

I've had black friends tell me they are tired of white people acting ignorant to the fact that racism still exists; they've had experiences when they felt mistreated because of the color of their skin. My black friends don't want to have their history *and* personal experiences ignored or brushed aside. I see you, my black friends. I get that, too.

All races deserve to be *seen*; they come to the table with different decks of cards and we need to be listening to both perspectives.

In the '60's, my Dad attended high school in Hightstown, New Jersey. During weeks of race rioting, a black gang tried to jump him in the hallway; he was grateful to a member of the gang, his friend, who stood up for him.

Conflicts between black and white people continued long past my dad's high school days. My husband grew up in a suburb of Philadelphia, where his high school was known for its lower economic population and its gifted basketball team.

Rob's senior year, he was the only white player on an otherwise all-black basketball team. He noticed that the same teammates he out-played during practice were often the players that started the game, while he waited for his turn from the bench. He couldn't help but wonder if his coach wasn't playing him because he was the white one, and stereotypically black players are believed to play basketball at a higher level. It was a frustrating season for him; he was grateful to an assistant coach who recognized the unfair treatment.

On the flip side, Rob witnessed his black teammates deal with harassment. He remembers one particular game when the opposing team (which came from a much wealthier and whiter high school) called his teammates racially charged terms on the court, like "monkey." Rob's coaches responded by inspiring the players to work that much harder. It worked; Rob's team won.

Yes, racism does still exist. Rob should have been played based on his skill level, not his skin color. And his teammates should not have been called names. Each player on that team deserved understanding.

We don't need to ignore skin color or act colorblind to achieve racial equality. We can acknowledge racism exists and validate the pain it's created; that is when healing begins.

GENDER EQUALITY

Growing up, I always wanted to be a boy. I liked getting dirty and playing with a ball. That's what it means to be a boy, right? I was little and life's answers were simple.

In an effort to appear as different from pink and frills as possible, I often wore baggy jean overalls and T-shirts. My mom would point out a nice pink shirt at the store and I'd gag. I remember how she used to attempt braids and bangs, only to have me put my head in the bathroom sink and slick my hair back down. I'm really sorry about that one, Mom.

As I reached my teenage years and all *those* hormones started kicking in, I was glad to be a girl. However, in an effort to be completely transparent, I must admit that somewhere back in the most private corners of my mind, I still naturally thought that boys were better than girls.

Where did that idea come from? Was it the culture I grew up around, movies I watched, or my relationships with family members? While I have some of the pieces to the puzzle, I don't know exactly why I thought boys were superior to girls.

Certainly our world history supports my inner turmoil over which gender is superior. In cultures around the world, women have been treated poorly based solely on their sex. The same can be said for race, sexual orientation, and other issues. Our history has written some uncomfortable, complicated, and horrific chapters. I am grateful to live in the time and place I do; many men and women sacrificed greatly for the rights I have today.

While I didn't always feel this way, I can confidently say that I love being a woman. I love stories of women who overcame, because I relate to them. I am a woman and I have overcome; I am drawn to similar narratives.

The "Me Too" movement, a campaign against sexual harassment and sexual assault of women, exploded across the internet in 2006. The movement wasn't started with a viral hashtag in mind; it was started in community centers, classrooms, and church basements to help young girls—survivors of sexual harassment and assault—know they were not alone.

I was inspired by the movement's founder, Tarana Burke, a survivor herself, when she explained the importance of telling our stories. She said,

> Who wants to look at the mess? Even as a black person, I would rather not think about racism and oppression. As a survivor, I would rather not think about the things that I don't have and the things that happened to me. I don't even want to think about them, so I know people who don't experience them don't want to think about them. But how do we live together if we're not privy to . . . hold space for everybody's experiences and . . . reality. How do we coexist? . . . If you can't hear me, then I think you can't see me.[47]

Whether we are male or female, the past *and* present tells us unsettling stories about our gender. We can acknowledge the stories and the reality that they exist. By validating pain, we can move forward with love for anyone hurt by the past and believe in our bright future *together*.

I'm sad when I see the media and other sources portray men as "less than." I recently noticed a picture on social media; it was a snapshot of a group of women standing outside a state capitol building. They held posters, one of which read, "When you educate a man, you educate a man. When you educate a woman, you educate a generation." In an effort to highlight the irreplaceable effect women have on our society, this statement puts men down.

Is it possible to have compassion for both men *and* women? Absolutely. We can amplify the strengths of men, while equally empowering women. Women *and* men deserve to have their voices heard; they are different from each other and what makes them different makes them *powerful*, not *competitors*.

I look up to my grandparents who treated each other as equals. Grandpa attended musicals with Grandma, who was a talented wedding singer. Grandma learned to golf for Grandpa, who years earlier helped build a golf course because his town didn't have one. They valued each other's strengths and differences. We can each strive to highlight the strengths of others, the way they did for each other.

No, boys aren't better than girls. And girls aren't better than boys.

Boys are boys. Girls are girls. People deserve to be heard, no matter their gender.

SEXUAL ORIENTATION EQUALITY

I have witnessed hearts heal as gay and straight people strive to understand each other.

"Coming out" is a metaphor for a gay person disclosing their sexual orientation. Dependent on many factors, coming out can be a vulnerable, even frightening experience. While there are many coming out stories, my friend Ben's is one of my favorites.

Ben spent much of his life wishing to be dead and straight, instead of being what he was: alive and gay. While he first recognized his attraction to men in sixth grade, his self-hatred kept him "in the closet" until he was twenty-three. The first time he came out, he was on a walk with his two straight friends. Both were men, and one of them happened to be his current roommate.

He said, "For as long as I can remember, I've been more attracted to men than women." In a moment of true genuine concern, Ben added, "I understand if you don't want to be my roommate anymore."

His friend responded, "Why wouldn't I want to be your roommate anymore? You're the same person you've always been."

This example of two men, one straight and one gay, being respectful of each other's sexual orientation, is moving. Ben was respectful of his straight friend's need to feel comfortable, and his friend answered him with love and acceptance. Having been filled with shame for so long, Ben said this about the exchange, "For me that was when my heart started to heal. Knowing that my friends weren't going to reject me, that they would be there for me."

As we love people, regardless of whether or not our sexual orientations are the same, we can remember the sentiment, by Fyodor Dostoyevsky, "Love makes people feel equal."

VALIDATION HEALS

The healing that comes from validation is real. When we listen and empathize with others, they're able to clear out mental space for growth. I learned this for myself. When I began processing out loud the complicated experiences from my childhood and had my feelings validated by others, my healing process was accelerated.

There is a reason the Pride Parade started. It's because gay people have been attacked in bathroom stalls and beaten to death. There is a reason we celebrate Black History Month. It's because black people were sold like property and treated like animals. There is a reason I love pump-me-up, girl power songs. It's because I've spent a lot of my life wondering if men are more capable than women. We all need love, validation, and a listening ear.

Validation is saying, "You are worth my time and love because you are a human being, whether I agree with you or not." While our compassion and connection won't heal *all* wounds (because we can't fix others), it is the best chance we have to soften hearts and create new beginnings where everyone gets a turn at the microphone. (*That's your cue, Michael Jackson—"I'm starting with the man in the mirror."*)

Listening to someone, in whatever chapter of life they find themselves, is a brilliant choice.

The Bottom Line

We can find common ground as we listen to each other. Validating someone's experience creates healing and the ability to move forward.

Part Six

Why It Matters

Chapter 19

Illuminating the Darkness

Come, Mr. Frodo! I can't carry it for you, but I can carry you.[48]

—Samwise Gamgee, *Return of the King*

I saw way too many scary movies as a kid.

One particular night, after my dad had convinced our entire family to watch Stephen King's *Rose Red*, I couldn't sleep. I kept replaying the scariest scenes of the movie in my mind. I left my bedroom, crawled through the dark, up the basement stairs, and found the kitchen. I figured if I was awake being scared I might as well eat. I heard something behind me and jumped. I turned around to see my older brother, Danny, wrapped up in a blanket, sitting on top of the heater vent in our living room; his eyes were as big as mine.

We were three years apart in age and miles apart in interests. I didn't like my brother, and he certainly didn't like me.

Sidenote: When I was five and he was eight, I threw a spoon at his head. My aim was impeccable. He still has an indent, square between his eyebrows, of which I am quite proud of.

"What are you doing up here?" I whispered.

"I'm scared! I can't move!" he said. "All I can think about is that one scene where that lady . . ." I'll spare you the nightmares.

After getting a tub of powdered hot cocoa and a spoon, I joined Danny at the heater vent. I got under the blanket and shared my snack. Although we fought during daylight hours, the darkness of the night brought us together. We huddled together over the warm heater vent until we got up the guts to go back to bed, or fell asleep there. I can't remember which.

Dire circumstances can help us connect with just about anybody. And by the time Danny hit high school, we were best friends.

The night of the scary movie, all of our past arguments faded into the background. The main priority was to get through the night; nothing else mattered besides surviving those hours, and our best chance was to do it together. In the same way, when someone is so deep in the hole that they've given up on ever getting out, nothing else matters but getting them through their dark night.

SUICIDE—BRINGING HOPE IN THE DARKEST HOURS

Any past disagreements, promises of privacy, or social norms become irrelevant when someone wants to end their life. Just like my fights with Danny no longer mattered on the night of the heater vent, anything keeping us from protecting someone from suicide should fade into the background. This leaves the main priority, which is helping someone survive the night.

In severe situations, a person's turmoil may push them to their absolute limit. Outside help becomes crucial. When someone has been isolated for too long, they might not believe there is a way out. They need someone who is willing to sit with them through the night, assuring them that the sun will rise in the morning.

While the thoughts were many, I made a plan for suicide only once.

A combination of my psychological depletion and a medication error resulted in a night where my brain began to engage in the unthinkable. My mind was broken when I resolved to take my life.

That night, suicide made complete sense in my head; it felt like a good idea. I wasn't a person who wanted to cause pain for my family; I was a person who didn't have all engines firing properly. So it is with everyone who makes a plan for suicide; that's why they make the plan—because they aren't thinking properly. Victims of suicide deserve love and compassion.

I did not follow through with my plan. I am grateful that something in me pierced through the darkness to say, *Something is wrong. This isn't me.* I woke up Rob to the worst night of his life. He held my hand as we got the help I needed. We fought the darkness together and we love each other for it.

I know what can happen when someone loses hope; I have been that person. There are people I love, who aren't here to tell their story because the darkness swallowed them. I wish they could have found hope and made a different choice. While I boldly say that suicide is always a mistake, I have compassion for someone who makes that choice; I just wish they had chosen differently because our world needs them and hope can be found here.

When Robin Williams died by suicide, a popular meme circulated the internet with the phrase, "Genie, you are free." I don't think that's the message we should be sending to people and I don't believe suicide is the freedom that expression insinuates. What I do believe is there is hope and healing available in the next life for those who die by suicide.

WHAT THE NUMBERS SAY

Suicide has become everyone's problem.

Recent statistics show that suicide is the tenth leading cause of death in the US, and the *second* leading cause of death for people ages ten through thirty-four. Americans die by suicide an average of 129 people per day. For every one completed suicide, there are twenty-five attempts. Based on those numbers, that means 3,225 people try to kill themselves everyday in the United States alone. The rising numbers are horrifying.[49]

If we haven't personally been affected by a suicide, we know someone who has. Adults, teenagers, and even children are falling victim to the lie that suicide promises.

Through my own experiences and the experiences of others, I'll offer a few thoughts on the most tragic response to isolation and how we can help.

When someone wants to commit suicide, they don't necessarily want to die. Usually, they want to be free of the negative emotions they are feeling. Given the right support and tools, freedom can be found in staying alive.

There *is* hope. Suicide is one of the most preventable kinds of death and almost *any* positive action can save a life. As we understand the tools we can use to *see* someone who's contemplating suicide, we can literally save their life.

TALK, THEN LISTEN

Studies show that asking someone directly about their suicide intent usually lowers their anxiety and the risk of an impulsive action by them.

To ensure that someone in the dark is safe, we need to ask direct questions like, "Do you ever think about hurting yourself?" or more specifically, "Have you thought about suicide?" We can ask compassionate follow-up questions to help us understand their current mentality.

We can listen. Listen. And listen some more. If the person doesn't feel like talking, we can pull up a chair and sit with them during their night. Our willingness to listen and *be* can rekindle hope and make all the difference for someone trapped in the hole.

And while I don't recommend plain hot cocoa powder specifically, bringing a snack along is never a bad idea.

We can validate feelings of pain and let people know that we love them without conditions. I know from personal experience that it can be a scary thing to admit to someone you are having dark, intrusive thoughts. It can make you feel humiliated, weak, and selfish. Providing compassion is vital to empathizing with someone in the dark.

SOUND THE ALARM

Ask the person, "Will you go with me to get help?"

Suicidal people often don't believe they can be helped, so we can call in reinforcements. Just like Sam screamed when the stroller—with his baby sis in it—was rolling towards traffic, we can sound an alarm so others can rush to help.

The best option for getting a suicidal person help is taking them directly to someone who can help them. The next best option is to get a commitment from them to accept help; then we can make the arrangements for them. If nothing else, we can ask for a commitment from them that they won't commit suicide until we get them help.

Darkness can make it nearly impossible to see and think clearly. A person, immersed in the pitch black of night, can come to believe that the pain will never end and others would be better off without them. Suicide is usually an act, not of selfishness, but of desperation from someone who cannot see another way out.

NEVER UNDERESTIMATE OUR INFLUENCE

We never know who could be contemplating suicide. It could be our co-worker, a neighbor, our kid's friend, or a stranger at the gas station. We can provide hope to the people having these thoughts by embodying compassion. A smile or a kind comment can provide a moment of light for someone lost in the dark.

A line in *Dear Evan Hansen*, an inspiring broadway musical, says, "No one should flicker out or have any doubt that it matters that they are here. No one deserves to disappear."[50]

Suicide is not a hopeless cause. It is preventable. Seeing people with compassion and connecting with them is a powerful antidote against suicide. Light has the power to *always* overcome the darkness.

There is meaning to be had in life, no matter how dark the night.

The Bottom Line

Compassion and connection save lives from the darkest nights. While other resources are vital, nothing can take the place of human compassion and connection to give someone hope until morning comes.

Chapter 20

Meaning in Our Suffering

I have been in a place for six incredible years, where winning meant a crust of bread and to live another day. Since the blessed day of my liberation I have asked the question, "Why am I here?" [51]

—Gerda Weissmann Klein, Holocaust Survivor

Growing up, I was fascinated with the Holocaust and the events that unfolded. I read all the Holocaust young adult literature I could get my hands on: *Number the Stars, The Devil's Arithmetic,* and *The Diary of Anne Frank.* I was amazed at the heroism these brave characters embodied, and especially their human kindness amidst their suffering.

As an adult, I am still in awe of these heroes. I especially love Viktor Frankyl's story. Frankyl was a psychiatrist who survived a Nazi death camp and he outlined his experiences from both a practical and psychological standpoint in his memoir, *Man's Search for Meaning.* One of the lessons I learned from Viktor Frankyl's book, is that human kindness can be found in almost any situation, no matter how dire. Frankyl wrote about a time a prison guard gave him a piece of bread. "It was far more than the small piece of bread which moved me to tears at the time. It was the human 'something' which this man also gave me—the word and look which accompanied the gift."[52]

Amidst his suffering, Frankyl was able to find meaning in his suffering. Instead of isolating himself from human connection, he was able to recognize the goodness of others, which helped him see beyond the concentration camp. Finding meaning in his suffering helped him survive and help others.

See beyond the concentration camp. Those words came to my mind during a challenging weekend, just six months ago.

AN OPPORTUNITY TO FIND MEANING

Even in darkness it is possible to create light.[53]

—Elie Wiesel

I was strangely emotional one day. I found myself yelling and crying in spurts. As the day wore on, I felt nauseated and dizzy. Was it the giant peanut butter chocolate cookie I had just eaten? Or the even bigger soda I threw back with it? I felt seriously ill. When Rob got home from work that evening, he told me to lie on the couch and he took care of our two kids. We discussed the possibility of the flu. That evening, I began to emotionally unravel—I hadn't spiraled that badly in years. The antidepressant I took kept me from falling through this trap door of horror. Why wasn't it working? So much crying, so much self-hate talk, and Rob was driving me crazy by trying to fix it. We hadn't dealt with one of my anxiety episodes for a while and we were both out of practice.

I went to one of the two places I go when I am feeling overstimulated or down. The tub or the shower. That day's sanctuary was the tub.

All I could think was, *I thought we were done with this.* Heck, I was *speaking* to people about thriving in their mental health, and here I was, hanging onto mine by a thread.

I sat in the tub, watching the water pour on my feet in a rhythm that matched my racing thoughts. I tried to remember all of the tools I had learned over the years in therapy. I tried to *see* myself.

I talked to myself the way I would talk to a friend. "You're ok, Honey." I rubbed my hand back and forth over my collar bone to comfort myself. "You're alright. It's okay that you feel scared. You're going to be ok." There is nothing quite like speaking to my inner child—the one who is terrified of anxiety, depression, and the lie that her life is over when she feels anything like it. Self-compassion is a powerful tool against fear.

A thought came to the forefront of my mind.

See beyond the concentration camp.

I felt like I was in my own concentration camp, imprisoned in my own personal hell—my mind. What did I need to do to get through this night?

See beyond the concentration camp. Like Frankyl and other holocaust survivors, I needed to find meaning and purpose in my suffering.

At 11:45 p.m., *my purpose* found me in a ball of tears. And this time, he didn't try to fix it.

Rob, who desperately needs sleep to avoid migraines, came to me and held me while I sobbed in his arms. He didn't say anything; he knew he just needed to be there with me. It's not the first time Rob has seen me with that kind of gentleness.

His love roared louder than her demons. I've never been able to find who said that, but the moment I saw it, I thought of my Rob. Our first ten years of marriage have not been easy, but they have certainly been meaningful.

We don't like to cuddle much at night because it's just too hot and Rob turns over in his sleep every five minutes, so spooning sessions are short or non-existent. But that night he held me and he didn't move a muscle. As someone who makes a hobby out of preventing bad things from happening (the people that know him are laughing right now), Rob has been forced to come to grips with the harsh reality that he cannot protect me from my thoughts. He can't fix it and he hates it so much. But he does what he can; he makes sure I know that I am not alone. When things fall apart, he knows his job is to hold me. His human kindness pushed me forward through my sleepless night.

I called a few of my friends in tears the next morning. They supported me with words of encouragement. At breakfast, I pulled out my pill calendar to take my antidepressant and vitamins.

I stopped. I stared. I couldn't believe what I was seeing.

There were pills sitting in the last two days' compartments. The wheels in my brain began to spin. The antidepressant I take is effective, but high maintenance; it is supposed to be taken the same time every day or the side effects can mess with your head. I had forgotten to take my medicine for *two days*.

Everything started making sense: the lightheadedness, the nausea, the uncontrollable anxiety, the insomnia, all of it! There was a concrete reason why I was suffering so much. My anti-depressant *did* still work, but I hadn't been taking it.

Within a few days of taking the medication again, the chemicals in my brain balanced and I began to feel at ease. I was back to my able-to-handle-life self within the week.

It would be easy to write off my stupid mistake and subsequent awful weekend, but suffering is suffering is suffering.

There is meaning to be had in every experience.

EMPATHY

> For the first time in my life I saw the truth as it is set into
> song by so many poets, proclaimed as the final wisdom
> by so many thinkers. The truth—that love is the ultimate
> and the highest goal to which man can aspire.[54]
>
> —Viktor Frankl

I was waist-deep in the hole that weekend, and I hated it. But I was also reminded of what being in the hole feels like and it strengthened my empathy for others.

When my next-door neighbor lost her father suddenly to a heart attack a few months later, I cried. Not because I had lost a parent; I hadn't. I cried because I had been sobbing in the tub a few months earlier. Because I was familiar with pain, I felt compassion for the hurt she was feeling. Suffering teaches us empathy. Empathy is compassion, a compassion that drives us toward each other to make a connection.

There are people all around us who want to understand and whose love comes without conditions. It doesn't matter if they've had the same struggles we've had. Their own experiences give them a capacity to understand and to love.

HUMAN KINDNESS

> In spite of everything, I still believe
> that people are really good at heart.[55]
>
> —Anne Frank

I was reminded of human kindness during my difficult weekend. Rob and the friends I called in tears all responded with compassion.

One of them was my same friend who would lose her dad two months later.

I watched my neighborhood rally around her. People walked her dog, watched her kids, and brought her family dinner. Her husband told me, "You know, these kinds of experiences remind you that while there is a lot of bad in this world, most people are awesome."

It is sometimes in our suffering that we are able to witness the best humanity has to offer. We are able to recognize what *seeing* really looks like, and the experience serves as an education to help us do the same.

A NOTE TO THE READER

Reader, I don't know where your life is at right now. Maybe your life feels happy, peaceful, exciting. I certainly hope so. Or maybe your life feels confusing, complicated, and uncertain. That's okay too.

Or maybe you are in the middle of your own concentration camp. I'm sorry. I see you, Friend.

Wherever you are on life's journey, I want to tell you that there is hope. If you give it time, light always, always, always comes and dispels darkness. The light is brighter because you understand the darkness.

There is meaning in pain. It teaches us empathy and human kindness; it empowers us to save. People need us and the perspective our challenges bring. Just like my sister texted me during my weekend of sans-medication, "Hang in there."

Challenges are part of the give-and-take of life. If we allow it, periods of suffering can refine our ability to see others; to see them better than before.

We can do hard things and our experiences will make us more capable of saving others. All life is meaningful and miracles are on their way.

The Bottom Line

Suffering is meaningful when it creates empathy and helps us recognize human kindness. All life experiences can teach us lessons that help us see others.

Chapter 21

The Miracle

"I don't believe in God."
"It doesn't matter.
He believes in you." [56]

—*The Count of Monte Cristo*

Do you remember the girl on the bathroom floor? It's been a while. Mary Poppins didn't come to save me and my children. I had to show up for myself that day.

I mustered all my emotional energy, peeled myself off the floor, and did what needed to be done.

I played Candy Land with my kids.

I washed dishes.

I took baths.

I called my sisters when I couldn't take another minute.

I did One. Thing. At. A. Time.

I knew I was waiting for a miracle. What I didn't know was that the miracle would come through everyday people. People who were rested and ready to take the log off my shoulder.

On one of these bathroom floor days, I called out to my neighbor for help. She was a woman in her mid-60's who loved Diet Pepsi and gardening in her sunhat. I texted her, *I need you, can you help me?*

She was at my front door in moments. I crumpled into her chest. She dragged me over to the couch. She wrapped me up in her arms and cradled me like a child. She stroked my face and my hair as I sobbed. I told her I couldn't do it another day. I couldn't live like this. She understood.

She confided in me that she had experienced her own brand of hell in her young adulthood. She described how she wanted to give up; her narrative matched my reality now.

"You can do this," she told me. She helped me put on my kids' clothes and shoes so I could get out of the house for a walk. She *saw* me.

That's what we do when we see a person lying on their proverbial bathroom floor. We scoop them up in our arms, we hold them, and we listen to them sob until they can't sob anymore. We become their hope that day, their lighthouse amidst a turbulent storm. We become the miracle they have been begging for, praying for. We can be just enough to get them through a little longer, until their next miracle arrives. A miracle like mine.

I was sitting at the kitchen table, writing in my journal when it happened. I was hiding my face so my kids wouldn't see me crying if they walked by. Sam came over and started tapping my arm, saying something over and over again. At two-years-old, his sentences were garbled and unclear. After I composed myself, I said "What Sam?" He then said a phrase he had never spoken before, and a phrase I will never forget.

"Mommy. Jesus loves you."

Then he nonchalantly toddled away to play with the toys that were waiting for him.

I looked towards the ceiling and wept. I was trying to hide my face in the kitchen that day, but someone bigger than me still *saw me.* God made sure I knew He was there, even if He wasn't healing me the way I wanted.

When we feel overwhelmed by the amount of need we see around us, we can remember that it's not all up to us. We are a help, we are a light, and we are needed. We are miracles, even. But there is something much bigger than us that will pick up the pieces and mend the broken hearts.

We are here to provide the love sandwiches.

We are here to live in Whoville.

We are here to be different and powerful.

We are here to shine as leaders and friends.

We are here to remind people they are never alone.

We are here to sit with someone when nothing can fix it.

We are here to laugh in funny moments.

We are here to slow down.

We are here to illuminate the darkness.

We are here to create miracles, *together*.

In the words of Helen Keller, "I long to accomplish a great and noble task, but it is my chief duty to accomplish small tasks as if they were great and noble."[57] Our offering is enough.

This *seeing* business—are we going to get it right every time? Are we going to say and do things perfectly? No way. And that's okay. We will try again. And again. And again. And again.

We try to connect; we try to show compassion; we do *something*.

Doing *something* is what seeing people is all about. All our *something*s are a part of a much bigger *everything*.

What can we say to the woman on the bathroom floor?

Or the five-year-old who wants to fix her dad's depression?

We can get down on our knees at her level, and we can look into her eyes so she knows she is seen. We can whisper, *You are not alone, because I am right here. I am rooting for you.*

And sweetheart, I see you.

Endnotes

1. Idina Menzel, "I See You," *Idina* (Warner Bros., 2016).

2. Beverly Clark (Susan Sarandon), *Shall We Dance?*, directed by Peter Chelsom, produced by Simon Fields (Miramax Films, 2004).

3. Brené Brown, *Daring Greatly* (New York: Gotham/Penguin, 2012).

4. Dr. Seuss, *How the Grinch Stole Christmas* (New York: Random House, 1957).

5. Ibid.

6. Ibid.

7. Ibid.

8. Benj Pasek and Justin Paul, "You Will Be Found," from the Broadway musical *Dear Evan Hansen*, by Steven Levenson (2015).

9. Henry Ford and Samuel Crowther, *My Life and Work* (Garden City, NY: Doubleday, 1922).

10. Kristin Neff, "The Space between Self-Esteem and Self-Compassion," Ted[x] Talks, YouTube, 2013. See youtube.com/watch?v=IvtZBUSplr4. Accessed July 15, 2020.

11. Tara Brach, *Radical Acceptance*, reprint edition (New York: Bantam, 2004).

12. Neff, "The Space between Self-Esteem and Self-Compassion."

13. Safire Rose, "She Let Go," 2003. She is releasing a poetry book soon but has not announced the date. She has announced the book title on

her website as *"She Let Go" and Other Poems Along the Path of Love by Safire Rose.* You can find the poem on her website: safire-rose.com/books-and-media/poetry/she-let-go.

14. Freya Stark, *Perseus in the Wind* (London: Cox & Wyman, 1984).

15. Brené Brown, "The Anatomy of Trust," speech delivered at UCLA's Royce Hall, 2015. See brenebrown.com/videos/anatomy-of-trust-video/. Accessed July 22, 2020.

16. Tweet by author Bob Goff on December 29, 2015.

17. Elizabeth Gilbert, *Big Magic: Creative Living Beyond Fear* (New York: Riverhead Books, 2016).

18. Tweet by author Chetan Bhagat, August 2019.

19. Robert Emmons, "Why Gratitude Is Good," *Greater Good*, Nov. 2010.

20. Jon Petz, *Significance in Simple Moments* (Columbus, OH: Bore No More Publishing, 2014).

21. Theodore Roosevelt, "Citizenship in a Republic" and "The Man in the Arena," speeches delivered in Paris France, 1910.

22. Donald Miller, *A Million Miles in a Thousand Years* (Nashville: Thomas Nelson, 2011).

23. Clint Pulver is a personal friend of mine. You can view a video that brings this story to life on his website: clintpulver.com/about/.

24. John Lennon, "Beautiful Boy (Darling Boy)," *Double Fantasy* (Geffen, 1980).

25. Maren Bain, "Miracles Everywhere," creative narrative writing story for sixth grade English class, January 17, 2020.

26. Henry David Thoreau, *The Writings of Henry David Thoreau*, 16 volumes (New York: Houghton, Mifflin, 1906), 191.

27. J. K. Rowling, *Harry Potter and the Prisoner of Azkaban* (New York: Scholastic, 2001).

28. C. S. Lewis, "On Living in an Atomic Age," essay, 1948; as quoted in "Find Solace in Faith over Fear and Family Discussion," Mercury One. See mercuryone.org/find-solace-in-faith-over-fear. Accessed July 15, 2020.

29. Ellen DeGeneres, *Seriously . . . I'm Kidding* (New York: Hachette/Grand Central Publishing, 2012).

30. Jerry Spinelli, *Love, Stargirl*, reprint edition (New York: Ember/ Random House, 2009).

31. Danielle Doby, *I Am Her Tribe* (Kansas City: Andrews McMeel Publishing, 2018).

32. *Finding Forreste*r, directed by Gus Van Sant (Columbia Pictures, 2000; Minnetonka, MN: Millcreek Entertainment, 2014), DVD.

33. See wellnesslabandclinics.com/blog/what-to-do-when-empathy-and -boundaries-collide. Accessed July 22, 2020.

34. Brené Brown, *Rising Strong*: *How the Ability to Reset Transforms the Way We Live, Love, Parent, and Lead*, reprint edition (New York: Random House, 2017).

35. Byron Katie, *Loving What Is*, reprint edition (New York: Three Rivers Press/Random House, 2003).

36. Jason Headley, "It's Not About the Nail," YouTube, 2013. See youtube. com/watch?v=-4EDhdAHrOg. Accessed July 15, 2020.

37. Jennie Taylor, Facebook post, Feb. 7, 2020. See facebook.com/ jennie.a.taylor/posts/10156783507482617.

38. Henri Matisse, *Jazz*, Harry N. Abrams edition (New York: George Braziller, 1983).

39. Mitchell Stephens, "History of Television." See nyu.edu/classes/stephens /History%20of%20Television%20page.htm. Accessed July 22, 2020.

40. Wikipedia.org, "1954 Rosebowl," en.wikipedia.org/wiki/1954_Rose_ Bowl. Accessed July 22, 2020.

41. Ibid., "High Definition Television in the United States," en.wikipedia. org/wiki/High-definition_television_in_the_United_States. Accessed July 22, 2020.

42. Erica Jong, *Fear of Flying*; 2d ed. (New York: Penguin/Berkley, 2003).

43. *928 Maya Angelou Quotes*, collected by Arthur Austen Douglas (UB Tech, 2019).

44. Brown, *Rising Strong*.

45. Dr. Seuss, "The Sneetches," *The Sneetches and Other Stories* (New York: Random House, 1961).

46. Harper Lee, *To Kill a Mockingbird* (New York: Harper, 2014).

47. "Tarana Burke and Brené on Being Heard and Seen," *Unlocking Us with Brené Brown*, podcast, posted March 22, 2020. See podcasts.apple. com/us/podcast/tarana-burke-and-brené-on-being-heard-and-seen/ id1494350511?i=1000469205706. Accessed July 22, 2020.

48. J.R.R. Tolkien, *Return of the King* (New York: Mariner Books, 2005), 233.

49. The American Foundation for Suicide Prevention. For more information, see afsp.org/suicide-statistics/. Accessed July 22, 2020. Other available sources are the websites of the Utah Department of Health (IBIS), the World Health Organization, the Utah Death Certificate Database, the U.S. Center of Disease Control, the Utah Violent Death Reporting System, and the Utah Department of Health Violence and Injury Prevention Program.

50. Steven Levenson, *Dear Evan Hansen*, paperback edition (New York: Theatre Communications Group, 2017).

51. Gerda Weissman Klein in her Oscar acceptance speech, 1996. The award was for Best Documentary (Short Subject). See youtube.com/watch? v=5zn-fPM4KS0.

52. Viktor E. Frankl, *Man's Search for Meaning* (New York: Simon & Schuster/Pocket Books, 1985), 108.

53. Elie Wiesel, *Open Heart* (New York: Random House/Schocken, 2015), 72.

54. Frankl, *Man's Search for Meaning*, 57.

55. Anne Frank, *Anne Frank's Tales from the Secret Annex: Including Her Unfinished Novel Cady's Life* (New York: Random House/Bantam Books, 2003).

56. Alexandre Dumas, *The Count of Monte Cristo*, abridged edition (Mineola, NY: Dover Publications, 2007).

57. Lois J. Einhorn, *Helen Keller, Public Speaker: Sightless But Seen, Deaf But Heard* (Westport, CT: Greenwood Publishing, 1998).

About the Author

Julie Lee is best known for her genuine nature as a speaker, podcaster, and friend. Branded as a "shaker," she speaks boldly about the psychological battles she has fought inside. These experiences give her perspective and compassion for anyone who struggles to find purpose and meaning in life. In a world that craves authenticity, Julie's podcast *I See You* has given hope and inspiration to thousands of listeners.

A former public school teacher, Julie received a bachelor's degree in elementary education from Brigham Young University, with a minor in teaching English as a second language.

Sharing her message that compassion and connection save lives continues to be one of the most meaningful adventures of Julie's life. She lives in Utah with her husband, Rob, and their two children, Samuel and Lydia.

Scan to visit

www.julieleespeaks.com